molecules

molecules

j. c. speakman

(James Clare)

Senior Lecturer in Physical Chemistry
The University of Glasgow

mc graw-hill book company
New York St. Louis San Francisco
Toronto London Sydney

molecules

Copyright © 1966 by McGraw-Hill, Inc. All Rights Reserved.
Printed in the United States of America. This book, or
parts thereof, may not be reproduced in any form without
permission of the publishers.

Library of Congress Catalog Card Number 65-22960

1 2 3 4 5 6 7 8 9 0   CN   7 3 2 1 0 6 9 8 7 6

foreword

Living organisms are, before all else, molecular structures. Many of their properties derive directly from the properties of their component molecules, and much of their organization involves general forces of molecular interaction. Indeed we are beginning to see that significant aspects of the architecture of the cell have their source in the self-organizing architectonic properties of molecules, not only such macromolecules as the proteins and nucleic acids, whose large size and consequent inertia encourage the spinning of organized structure, but such relatively small molecules as the phospholipids, which spontaneously form membranes hardly to be distinguished from those of the cell. One can scarcely hope to understand biological organization without cultivating an easy familiarity with the world of molecules as such.

What is needed here primarily is to develop intuitions, to begin to acquire a feeling for what molecules are like and what behavior to expect of them. I tell my students to try to feel like a molecule. If they can reach the point of saying to themselves, when up against some problem of molecular behavior, "What would I do if I were that molecule?"—then things are going well.

When I began some years ago trying to convey the substance of molecular structure and behavior to students in an introductory biology course, I learned a great deal from what I considered a masterpiece of exposition at this level, Dr. Speakman's "Introduction to the Electronic Theory of Valency."* With the simplicity and directness that only authority can command, Dr. Speakman manages in this book to make sense of chemistry—the level of sense that is particularly useful to those who need to launch out from such a base into other fields. After some years of sending my students to this earlier text, it occurred to me that Dr. Speak-

* Edward Arnold, London, 3rd edition, 1955.

v

man might be persuaded to write a book that fitted our needs
even more closely, in which the subject might be developed
throughout with particular emphasis on the molecules that principally compose organisms and their environments. This is that
book, and it fulfills admirably all that I had hoped from it.

I should like to say something finally of the place of this kind of
treatment in the teaching of biology. In my own introductory
course we begin at the level of the elementary particles, assemble
them into the atoms of the periodic system, then go into forces of
chemical combination and the structure of molecules, molecular
interactions, the structure and properties of macromolecules,
chemical reaction, enzymes, processes of cellular metabolism, and
so eventually reach the living cell. I think that this progression is
a valuable intellectual contribution in that it conveys to the students a unified view of the levels of material organization and the
sequence in which they developed—probably the most valuable
thing that one can bring to students in an introductory course in
science. There is, however, an important byproduct of teaching
the subject in this way. We take our students without regard to
their previous preparation. All of them have had science instruc-
tion in school, but some have never had a course in chemistry or
physics or biology; and we treat them all alike. By developing the
subject in this way, one teaches what students of biology need
most to know about molecules, their behavior and reactions, as
part of the progress of the story. I never stop to point out that
certain portions of the course are physics or chemistry, physical
chemistry, or biochemistry. The whole emphasis is on content and
continuity; we try to convey a sense of studying not the sciences,
but nature. I think that this book can make a great contribution
to all who wish to approach the subject in this way.

George Wald

preface

At the moment of writing, molecular structures are known for only two of the simpler proteins—myoglobin (with the related hemoglobin) and lysozyme. We lack detailed knowledge of the vast variety of large molecules which constitute the essential feature of living organisms. On the other hand, our knowledge of the structures of small molecules, and of many of moderate size, is now intimate and quantitative. From this knowledge we can draw reasonable inferences about the structures, behavior, and functions of the larger biological molecules. This is the theme of this book, as indeed it is of the whole series of monographs.

The book starts from the simplest ideas of atomic structure, goes on to consider the electronic mechanisms by which atoms combine to yield molecules, and describes something of our knowledge of the sizes and shapes of these molecules.

The author is a chemist, and inevitably writes from a chemical point of view; but the book is oriented toward molecules of biochemical interest. The reader is assumed to have an elementary knowledge of chemistry, but the treatment is everywhere descriptive rather than exact. No mathematical knowledge is assumed.

The author wishes to place on record the stimulation he has received from a correspondence with Professor Wald, the General Editor of the series.

J. C. Speakman

Sunday after Easter, 1965

contents

1

the molecular concept

[The atoms] move in the void and catching each other
up jostle together, and some recoil in any direction that
may chance, and others become entangled with one
another in various degrees according to the symmetry
of their shapes and sizes and positions and order, and
they remain together and thus the coming into being of
composite things is effected.

SIMPLICIUS, *De Caelo*

**early ideas
about atoms**   The notion that all material objects consist of minute, invisible
atoms is ancient. The above quotation reminds us of this; Simplicius wrote in the sixth century, but he was summarizing the
ideas of the Greek philosopher Empedocles, who had taught a
thousand years earlier. It also reminds us of the power of the
atomic theory. Though most objects appear to be continuous and
all of a piece, this might be an illusion. That they really consist
of minute particles would explain many familiar phenomena
which are otherwise hard to explain: dissolving one substance in
another (when their atoms intermingle), volatilizing a substance
(when the atoms fly off into the air), or compressing a substance
(when the atoms are forced to crowd more closely together).

But though early atomic theories did provide a useful background
for explaining phenomena, they could do it only in a general and
qualitative way. To be effective, they needed a more precise and
quantitative basis, and this they did not begin to have until
the time of John Dalton (1766–1844), the English chemist and
physicist. The difficulty was that the "atoms" of most familiar
substances—wood or stones or flesh—are very complicated indeed. Only when simpler systems came to be recognized and suitable methods were developed for their study could a firm, quan-
titatively based atomic theory be constructed.

For these reasons there is no very close correspondence between our present, very definitive atomic concept and the views of the Greek atomists. We can easily misunderstand the Greeks and read into their writings a greater prophetic truth than might be justified. For instance, some of the Greeks did not regard the atoms themselves as strictly material. Isolated atoms "in the void" were not matter; material objects were created only when large numbers of atoms clustered together.

atoms and molecules

We have not yet mentioned the word *molecule:* the distinction between atom and molecule became clear only very gradually. Without trying for precise definitions—which are always difficult in an experimental science and usually not important, so long as we have an effective working idea of what we mean by the terms— we may state that an *atom* is the smallest piece of a particular element which can exist and that a *molecule* is the smallest piece of a particular substance that can exist independently and still possess the properties of the substance.

Usually a molecule comprises a number of atoms, but this is not always so—in special cases the atom may also be the molecule. For instance, there are atoms of hydrogen and of oxygen, often represented by the chemical symbols H and O, respectively. These do not normally exist in isolation; instead, they combine with other atoms in various ways to yield molecules: two hydrogen atoms may combine to produce a molecule of ordinary hydrogen, H_2; or two hydrogen atoms may combine with an atom of oxygen to produce a molecule of water, H_2O. However, in some situations, as in the outer atmosphere of the sun, hydrogen exists as single atoms. Under these conditions the hydrogen molecule is simply the atom, H. Even under normal terrestrial conditions the inert gases, such as helium, exist as single atoms, and He therefore stands for both atom and molecule.

We can illustrate the difficulty of giving a watertight definition of the molecule by asking whether an ion can be considered as a molecule. As we shall see later, a salt such as sodium chloride consists of oppositely charged sodium and chloride ions, Na^+ and Cl^-. These exert a powerful general attraction on each other, but they do not normally pair off as discrete couples, Na^+Cl^-. So what is the molecule in this case?

the laws of chemical combination Dalton's achievement was to show that an atomic hypothesis provided a rational explanation of the laws of chemical combination. There are three of these laws:

1. *Constant proportions.* When two or more elements combine to give a particular compound, they do so in constant and definite proportions by weight. (We now know that this law is not always exactly obeyed. But it is very nearly obeyed in most compounds, and it is therefore a most valuable law for the practical chemist. This is another example of the unimportance of precise definition in science.)

2. *Multiple proportions.* When two elements combine to form two or more different compounds, the amounts of the one element that combine, in the different compounds, with a given amount of the other are themselves in a simple ratio.

3. *Reciprocal proportions.* When an element A forms compounds with either of two other elements D and E, and when D and E combine with each other to give a third compound, the proportions in which D and E separately combine with a given amount of A will also be the proportions in which they combine together.

These experimental laws, when at last they were established, were simply explained by assuming that the elements consisted of atoms—all of the same weight for a given element, but of different weights for different elements—and that compounds were formed by the union of definite numbers of atoms of each of the elements involved. When a compound contained just two elements, it was supposed that there would normally be one atom of each kind but that larger numbers might sometimes unite.

For instance, hydrogen and oxygen combine to form water in a ratio, by weight, of about 1:8. (More exactly, the ratio is now known to be 1:7.94.) Dalton supposed that the water molecule comprised one atom of each element, HO, and hence that the relative weights of the atoms were in this same ratio of 1:8. Later, various considerations led to the conviction that an atom of oxygen in fact combines with two atoms of hydrogen to form a molecule which we accordingly symbolize by H_2O. If this is so, the relative weights of the atoms must be as 1:16, so that the weights of hydrogen and oxygen combining are in the ratio of

$(2 \times 1):16 = 1:8$. Thus the law of constant proportions is accounted for.

The law of multiple proportions is similarly explained. Hydrogen and oxygen can also combine to yield hydrogen peroxide, in which the relative weights are as $(2 \times 1):(2 \times 16) = 1:16$. Comparing water with hydrogen peroxide, we find that the respective weights of oxygen combining with the same weight of hydrogen are as $1:2$. We represent the hydrogen peroxide molecule by the formula H_2O_2.

To illustrate the law of reciprocal proportions, we must consider three elements and at least three of their compounds. We may select hydrogen, oxygen, and carbon, and water, methane, and carbon dioxide. The molecules are now formulated as H_2O, CH_4, and CO_2. In H_2O, as we have seen, hydrogen and oxygen combine in the weight ratio $1:8$. If, for convenience, we specify our unit of weight as the gram, we may then state that 4 g of hydrogen combines with 32 g of oxygen. In methane, CH_4, 4 g of hydrogen combines with 12 g of carbon. In carbon dioxide, CO_2, 12 g of carbon combines with 32 g of oxygen, as the law of reciprocal proportions requires.

Carbon and oxygen also combine to form carbon monoxide, with the modern formula CO, in which the ratio of the elements is $12:16 = (2 \times 12):32$. To cover such cases, which are common, the third law needs amending to conclude as follows: ". . . the proportions in which D and E separately combine with a given weight of A will be equal to, *or in a simple ratio to*, the proportions in which they combine with one another." The ratio of the weights of oxygen united with a given weight of carbon in carbon dioxide and carbon monoxide is $2:1$.

atomic weights On this basis and with increasingly accurate methods of analysis, chemistry was able to develop extensively during the nineteenth century. To be sure, the absolute weights of the atoms were quite unknown for most of the century and were known only roughly toward its end. That atoms are extremely small and light and that weighable quantities of any element or compound must comprise an enormous number of individual atoms or molecules was certain.

table 1.1 **the atomic weights of some elements (based on $C^{12} = 12.0000$)**

ELEMENT	SYMBOL	ATOMIC NUMBER	ATOMIC WEIGHT
Hydrogen	H	1	1.00797
Carbon	C	6	12.01115
Nitrogen	N	7	14.0067
Oxygen	O	8	15.9994
Fluorine	F	9	18.9984
Sodium	Na	11	22.9898
Magnesium	Mg	12	24.312
Phosphorus	P	15	30.9738
Sulfur	S	16	32.064
Chlorine	Cl	17	35.453
Potassium	K	19	39.102
Manganese	Mn	25	54.938
Iron	Fe	26	55.847
Copper	Cu	29	63.54
Zinc	Zn	30	65.37
Iodine	I	53	126.904

For most chemical purposes, however, *relative* weights suffice, and thus a system of so-called *atomic weights* was set up. The weight of the atom of one particular element was chosen as standard, and the weights of all other types of atom were expressed relative to that standard. At one time the standard was the hydrogen atom, with a weight of 1. On this basis the atomic weight of oxygen was 15.88. Later the system was modified by taking oxygen as the standard with a weight of exactly 16, and this made the atomic weight of hydrogen 1.008.

About 1930 it was realized that ordinary oxygen contains three *isotopes;* besides O^{16}, the principal constituent, there are small but significant proportions of the heavier isotopes O^{17} and O^{18}. In consequence, two slightly different scales of atomic weights came into use: the *chemical scale,* based on 16.0000 for ordinary mixed-isotope oxygen, and the *physical scale,* based on 16.0000 for oxygen consisting of the commonest isotope O^{16} only. The difference between these two scales was small, though not negligible in accurate work; but since 1960, it has been resolved by adopting the principal isotope of carbon, C^{12}, as the standard with a weight of exactly 12. Table 1.1 lists current atomic weights for the elements that are most important in biological systems. Ordinary carbon also contains a heavier isotope C^{13}. Its proportion is small, however, as can be deduced from the fact that the mean atomic weight for carbon shown in Table 1.1 differs from 12 by only about 0.1%.

Reliance on relative atomic weights implied a theoretical difficulty which caused some early confusion. The water molecule came to be regarded as composed of three atoms, as indicated by the formula H_2O. How could chemists be sure that it was not in fact composed of six atoms, each of half the original weight, and that it should not properly be represented by the formula H_4O_2? Or why not halve the atomic weight of oxygen to yield a formula H_2O_2—or, more simply, HO, which was actually used by Dalton? (Hydrogen peroxide would then need to be formulated as H_2O_4 or, more simply, HO_2.)

During the nineteenth century, there was little direct evidence upon which to base an answer to such questions. Nevertheless, after much experimentation and lengthy controversy, answers were agreed upon. There were good inferential reasons for preferring H_2O to HO, and a decision between H_4O_2 and H_2O was based on the consideration that the latter was simpler and led to no serious inconsistencies. By 1860, most chemists had accepted a system of formulas substantially identical with that still in use. During the second quarter of this century, direct physical methods for studying molecular structure were developed, as we shall explain more fully in Chap. 4. The interesting thing is that, in nearly every case, the molecular formula based on chemical evidence proved to be correct. The water molecule really is H_2O.

chemical structure Having agreed that the molecule of water was validly represented by the formula H_2O, or that of carbon dioxide by CO_2, or that of acetic acid by $C_2H_4O_2$, chemists were next able to deduce something about the arrangement of these atoms within their respective molecules. At first this must have seemed an impossible task, since the molecules were much too small ever to be seen and since the information accessible was largely restricted to analyses of amounts of material containing huge, and unknown, numbers of actual molecules.

A first clue lay in the discovery of *isomerism:* the occurrence of different substances that were nevertheless represented by the same molecular formula. Besides acetic acid, another compound was found to have the formula $C_2H_4O_2$: methyl formate. This at once implied that these eight atoms could be arranged in at least two different ways; they were not just clumped together at random. There must be one particular arrangement of the eight atoms giving a molecule of acetic acid and another one giving a molecule of methyl formate. To suggest how this problem was solved, we shall give just one piece of evidence bearing on the arrangement in acetic acid.

Acidity was known to be associated with the presence of hydrogen atoms in the molecule, but it was restricted to only one of the four appearing in the formula $C_2H_4O_2$. When that atom was replaced by sodium to yield sodium acetate, $C_2H_3O_2Na$, the product was no longer an acid. Hence one hydrogen atom must be presumed linked to the rest of the molecule in a different way from the other three. By long efforts of this kind, detailed *structures* were gradually established for this and for many more complicated molecules. Instead of the mere molecular formula $C_2H_4O_2$, acetic acid could be more informatively represented by the structural formula (1). The molecules H_2O, H_2O_2, and CO_2 are similarly represented by (2), (3), and (4).

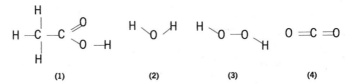

(1)   (2)   (3)   (4)

valence When a large number of structural formulas had become accepted, a new principle was recognized: each atom, according to its type, has a certain combining power which came to be known as its *valence*.* Carbon can always be represented with four links to other atoms. It has a valence of 4, or is quadrivalent. Oxygen normally has two links, and is bivalent. Hydrogen has one link, and is univalent.† The rule is that from every atom in a structural

---

* "Valence" is used in the United States; "valency" has been almost universal in Great Britain.

† Words such as "monovalent," "divalent," and "tetravalent" are often used and have become acceptable by usage. The termination "-valent" is of Latin origin, however, so that it is better not to prefix it with Greek numerals. Hence we prefer the following: uni-, bi-, tri- (or ter-), quadri-, quinque-, and sexavalent.

formula there must reach out as many *bonds* as corresponds to the valence number of the atom. To maintain this rule, *double bonds* are sometimes needed, as we see in formulas (1) and (4), and occasionally *triple bonds*.

These rules of valence were of the greatest use to chemists as they assigned formulas to more and more elaborate molecules. There were, indeed, certain complexities. Some elements appeared to have variable valences; iron, for instance, has valences of 2 and 3 in ferrous and ferric compounds, respectively. Again, where salts are concerned, we know that the original notion of valence is not so simply applicable as was at first supposed (see Chap. 3). However, simple valence numbers work extremely well for the elements hydrogen, carbon, nitrogen, and oxygen, and the molecules with which we are chiefly concerned in this book are made up of these elements. Respective attribution to these elements of valences 1, 4, 3, and 2 is a rule of great value and with few exceptions.

stereochemistry The formula (1) we gave for the acetic acid molecule is printed on paper, so that it is two-dimensional. For a period, such flat formulas were adequate to cover structural knowledge. Chemists of that earlier time would probably have admitted, if pressed, that the molecules must really be three-dimensional; but, they would have added, nothing was known of the true spatial shapes of molecules, so that speculation on the subject would be pointless. But here again a fuller knowledge of chemical behavior ultimately forced chemists to adopt a more detailed view of their own formulas.

To take a simple example, methane, CH_4, was written with the flat formula (5). Some, or all, of the hydrogen atoms in methane can be replaced by chlorine atoms; so that, among others, a compound can be prepared with the formula CH_2Cl_2 (dichloromethane). For such a molecule two different flat structural formulas, (6) and (7), can be written. In fact, only one dichloromethane can be prepared. Therefore, either the molecules are flat (as written), but one of the isomers is for some reason unobtainable, or (6) and (7) are really the same formula when viewed properly in three dimensions. In 1874, the French chemist J. A. le Bel and the Dutch chemist J. H. van't Hoff independently proposed a

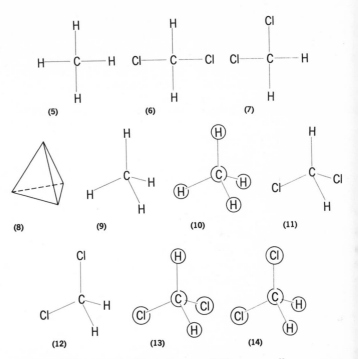

theory which covered this latter possibility, as well as a great many other facts that had awaited explanation. They proposed that the four valence bonds from a carbon atom are really directed toward the corners of a tetrahedron, which, if it is a regular tetrahedron, is the geometrical figure sketched in (8). Methane would then be more properly represented by a formula such as is suggested by (9), or, in a different convention, by (10). If this were true, then the three-dimensional versions of (6) and (7) would indeed be identical, as is seen in (11) and (12), or, more obviously in the other convention, in (13) and (14). A reorientation of (11) or (13) would bring it into a position in which it would be indistinguishable from (12) or (14).

The division of chemistry known as *stereochemistry* was thus founded; "Chemistry in Space" was the title of a book on the subject by van't Hoff. As it developed, the shapes of very complicated molecules were deduced by reasoning based almost wholly on chemical evidence. Glucose, a sugar, is a good example, though a simple one. The molecular formula is $C_6H_{12}O_6$, and a considerable number of isomeric *hexoses* with this same formula are known. In particular, a number of stereochemical variants are possible, and it was the achievement of the German chemist Emil Fischer (1852–1919) to assign the appropriate stereochemical formula to each sugar.

A molecule of ordinary glucose has the structure indicated by (15). [Glucose, in fact, exists in two slightly different modifications, and formula (15) corresponds to the β form. This formula also incorporates a structural detail that was unknown in Fischer's time.] There is a six-membered ring consisting of five carbon atoms and an oxygen, and in the diagram this is presented from rather above an edge-on view. These six atoms do not lie all in one plane; the ring is puckered. Most of the carbon atoms carry a hydrogen atom and a hydroxyl group, OH. The particular "up or down" arrangement of H and OH shown at each carbon is specific for glucose; if it were reversed at any place, the molecule would then correspond to another, different sugar. The detailed structures assigned to such molecules were based on chemical reasoning, but nearly all of them turned out to be correct when more direct, physical evidence became available.

molecular dissymmetry

When we look at our own right hand in a mirror, the image we see is of a left hand. If it were possible to take the image out of the mirror, we could not superpose it on the real right hand; it could not wear a right-hand glove.

The same effect can be seen with some molecules. For instance, in (16) we have redrawn the glucose molecule as it might appear in a mirror placed between it and (15). By no process of turning or twisting can formula (16) be made to look exactly like (15); the two are related as is an object to its mirror image, and they

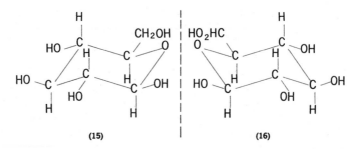

(15)   (16)

cannot be superposed. They differ only in handedness, or—to use a technical term now generally accepted—in *chirality*.

This difference of chirality is illustrated in a simpler way by any molecule in which the four atoms linked to one carbon atom are all different [e.g., (17)]. The mirror image (18) is not superposable on (17). Such molecules are said to be *dissymmetric*. The carbon atom carrying the four different atoms is said to be *asymmetric*. On the other hand, as the reader should check for himself, a molecule such as (11) is not dissymmetric; its mirror image is identical with the original molecule.

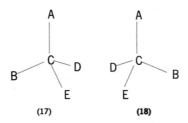

(17)   (18)

Since formulas (17) and (18), like (15) and (16), represent different molecules, they must correspond to different substances; but since the difference in structure is subtle, we should expect any difference in properties to be slight. For a difference to become evident the substance must in fact be placed in a dissymmetric environment. The simplest way to do this is to use polarized light. We need not go into the technical details here, except to state that one of the substances will twist, or rotate, the plane of polarization of the light clockwise and the other counterclockwise. An instrument for measuring this effect is known as a *polarimeter'* and it is a familiar piece of equipment in a chemical laboratory. The phenomenon was studied by Louis Pasteur (1822–1895),who gave it a general molecular explanation. A more detailed explanation, along the lines suggested above, became possible in terms of the theory of the tetrahedral carbon atom.

The substance which rotates the plane of polarized light clockwise is known as the *dextro isomer;* the other is the *levo isomer*. The prefix "dextro" signifies right-handed, and it is sometimes shortened to *d-* or replaced by +. "Levo" signifies left-handed, and it is shortened to *l-* or replaced by −.

Nearly all biologically important molecules are large enough to include at least one asymmetric carbon atom and so be dissymmetric. Only one of the two possible isomers is likely to occur naturally; sometimes it is the *d* isomer, sometimes the *l* isomer. For example, glucose as it occurs in plants is always *d*-glucose. The other isomer, *l*-glucose, can be made artificially, but it is useless as food, since no animal can digest it.

We have said that a dissymmetric environment is necessary to distinguish differences between dissymmetric molecules. The animal can very properly be regarded as such an environment, since nearly all the molecules which constitute its body are dissymmetric and—for each type—of one particular chirality. Therefore, differences between *d* and *l* isomers reveal themselves when these substances are introduced into the animal: one can be digested, the other cannot; one may be very poisonous, the other less so or not at all. We may take another simple example: the amino acid serine, represented by formula (19), has a dissymmetric molecule. In this case it is exclusively the *l* isomer that occurs in proteins. The *d* isomer can be made in the laboratory but does not occur naturally.

Until recently it was not certain which molecular configuration actually applied to a given *d* compound and which to the *l*. We did not know whether formula (15) or (16) truly represented the molecule of ordinary glucose, which rotates polarized light clockwise. This problem was solved in 1951 for tartaric acid by a sophisticated application of x-ray analysis (see page 60), and now the *absolute configurations* of all important dissymmetric molecules can be inferred. Formula (15) in fact turns out to be the correct one for ordinary glucose.

It sometimes happens that closely related molecules are known to have the same absolute configuration, yet rotate the plane of polarized light in opposite directions. For example, *d*-glyceraldehyde (20) can be proved to have the same configuration as *l*-lactic

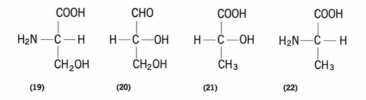

(19)   (20)   (21)   (22)

acid (21). (In these formulas we adopt the convention that the atoms or groups to the right and left of the central carbon atom are nearer to the viewer, while the groups above and below are farther away.) In order to stress the configurational relationship, such compounds are usually denoted by prefixing the small capital letters D or L, which can be used irrespective of whether the actual rotation of the light is d ($+$) or l ($-$).

Any substance whose actual molecular configuration can be shown to correspond to that of d-glyceraldehyde is said to belong to the D series. Thus, ordinary lactic acid (21) would be catalogued as D-(l)-lactic acid, or—preferably avoiding the unnecessary confusion—as D-($-$)-lactic acid. All the naturally occurring amino acids that have dissymmetric molecules belong to the L series, in the sense that their molecules have the configuration corresponding to l-glyceraldehyde, though many of them (unlike l-serine) have a positive rotation. An example is L-($+$)-alanine, with formula (22).

A biological system in which all the dissymmetric molecules are of the other chirality, ($-$)-glucose, ($+$)-serine, ($-$)-alanine, etc., is conceivable. Such a system would be incompatible with that existing on earth. According to a current hypothesis, life may have arisen on the earth spontaneously. We know that simple organic molecules may be formed from primary inorganic substances, such as water, carbon dioxide, ammonia, and hydrogen, under the influence of ionizing radiations. It is possible that a chance combination of such simple molecules could produce larger, protein-like molecules which might have some rudimentary property of reproducing themselves—of being "alive." Perhaps one molecule of this kind, among millions of failures, succeeded in establishing itself and became the basis for a process of organic evolution. If that happened, there would be a 50:50 chance of the system's having the chirality of its molecules one way or the other.

In the vastness of the universe it is likely that there are other planets very like our own. If the theory of the spontaneous formation of life is correct, then life will have developed on other planets too. Statistically, half of them should have life with the chirality opposite to that of our own. Their grass would look just as green as ours, but earthly cattle could not feed on it. Their cattle might look very like ours, but the earthly astronaut would die of starvation if he depended on their meat for sustenance.

the sizes of molecules

The table of atomic weights is based on the relative masses of the atoms. It was developed, and can be used, without any knowledge of the absolute masses. Structural chemistry progressed satisfactorily without more than the roughest idea of the actual masses or sizes of the molecules it so intimately described. Formulas such as (15) were valid as expressions of the compositions and properties of compounds. But no one had ever seen the molecule, and it seemed extremely unlikely that anyone ever would.

In this situation cautious chemists often warned their students against taking molecules too seriously. A structural formula was a useful shorthand device for summarizing how an actual material behaved. To feel any conviction that such a molecule "really existed," whatever that might mean, would be to push an hypothesis too far.

However, as more and more details were discovered, a simpleminded belief in the reality of molecules became harder and harder to resist. To most chemists today this detailed knowledge gives the molecule a familiarity which renders it as real as most other things in our strange universe. To recount some of the details of molecular architecture is a principal object of this book. In this introductory chapter we shall mention two features of the molecule: its mass and its overall size.

According to an hypothesis formulated by the Italian chemist Amadeo Avogadro, equal volumes of gases, under the same conditions of temperature and pressure, contain equal numbers of molecules. In line with this hypothesis, and indeed an implication of the Daltonian atomic theory itself, is the idea that chemically equivalent amounts of substances must contain equal numbers of molecules, or at any rate, numbers that are in a simple ratio. For instance, 2 g of hydrogen reacts with 16 g of oxygen to yield 18 g of water, a fact that we represent by the chemical equation

$$H_2 + \tfrac{1}{2} O_2 \rightarrow H_2O$$

Hence the number of actual molecules in the 2 g of hydrogen and in the 18 g of water must be exactly the same, and the number in 16 g of oxygen is just half as many.

The quantity of any substance which amounts to its molecular weight in grams is known as the *mole* (or mol or sometimes gram-molecule). Such quantities are the 2 g of hydrogen and the 18 g of water, while 16 g of oxygen is half a mole. The actual number of molecules in the mole of any substance must then always be the same. Because of its connection with the hypothesis, this important constant of nature is now known as the *Avogadro number*, and it is represented by the symbol N.

In rather a different guise, a value for this number was estimated by the Austrian physicist Joseph Loschmidt in 1865. Since this first, rough approximation, a variety of methods of increasing accuracy have been applied, and we now know the value of N to within one part in about 40,000. The current value, based on the C^{12} scale of atomic weights, is 6.0226×10^{23} molecules/mole. The reader may find it useful to remember this number in the rough-and-ready approximation of 6×10^{23}.

Given a reliable value of N, we can easily calculate the absolute mass of any specified molecule. Glucose, $C_6H_{12}O_6$, has a molecular weight of 180 (omitting the fraction). Therefore, 180 g of this compound constitutes the mole and so must contain N actual molecules. The weight of each molecule is thus

$$180 \div (6 \times 10^{23}) = 30 \times 10^{-23} = 3 \times 10^{-22} \text{ g}$$

We now make a rough estimate of the size of this molecule. The density of crystalline glucose is 1.56 g/cm³. Let us think of a small piece of this sugar, cubic in shape and with each of its edges 1 mm. Its volume would be 1 mm³, or 10^{-3} cm³. It would therefore weigh 1.56×10^{-3} g, and it would contain $(1.56 \times 10^{-3}) \div (3 \times 10^{-22})$ individual molecules. This works out to 5.2×10^{18}. For simplicity we now picture each molecule as a minute cube. Though this is not likely to be correct, it will not affect our rough estimate of size. We should then need to stack 5.2×10^{18} of these small cubes together to build our cubic piece of sugar with 1-mm edges. There would be $\sqrt[3]{5.2 \times 10^{18}} = 1.7 \times 10^6$ of them in every row of molecules along each edge of the cube. A single molecule would therefore occupy a frontage of $0.1 \div (1.7 \times 10^6) =$ about 6×10^{-8} cm. This value is an upper limit for the average width, or length, of the glucose molecule.

units of length for molecules

When we state values for the dimensions of molecules, we constantly find ourselves, as above, using 10^{-8} cm, a hundred-millionth of a centimeter. The centimeter is thus an inconveniently large unit for describing the sizes of molecules, and we generally use a smaller unit. By far the commonest is that suggested by the Swedish spectroscopist A. J. Ångström (1814–1874) for expressing the wavelengths of light. (The pronunciation, in Swedish, is approximately "Ongstrum.") This unit is known as the *Angstrom unit*, or *angstrom*, and it is represented by the symbol Å. We shall take 1 Å to be 10^{-8} cm. Until fairly recently this was not exactly true, though the error was wholly negligible for nearly all purposes. The angstrom was defined by the wavelength of a certain spectral line, while the meter (and hence the centimeter) was defined by the distance between two marks upon a particular bar of metal kept in Paris. But now we define the meter by direct reference to the wavelength, so that our definition of the relationship between angstrom and centimeter becomes exact.

Our rough estimate of the size of the glucose molecule would thus be expressed as 6 Å. We shall use this unit throughout this book, and the reader should accustom himself to thinking of molecules on this scale.

A unit of 10^{-7} cm, which is 10 times larger than the angstrom, is sometimes used for describing very large molecules, and often for colloidal particles. This is known as the *millimicron* and symbolized as mμ: 1 mμ = 10 Å.

gases, liquids, and solids

In the solid, crystalline state the molecules of a substance are relatively close together, and the regular outward shapes of crystals indicate that they are stacked in a regular way. Without at this stage defining our terms explicitly (see page 99, however) we may state that the molecules are "in contact" with their neighbors. If we think of a number of eggs packed regularly side by side in one tray of a crate and of a number of these trays piled regularly one on top of another, we have a fair analogy of the way the molecules might be packed in a crystal. There are obvious and important differences. First, instead of a crate containing perhaps a gross or two of eggs, we have a crystal which, even if it is very small to the eye, will comprise perhaps 10^{18} molecules. Second, the molecules are, so to say, in contact; there is no packing material between them. Third, unlike the eggs, the molecules do not stay still; they are always vibrating about their mean positions. Despite this vibration, however, the molecule normally continues to occupy its own site; only very occasionally does it vibrate so far as to exchange sites with a neighbor.

Liquids have densities that are generally lower than those of the corresponding solids. But the difference in density is small, and the molecules occupy sites that are only slightly farther apart, on the average, than those in the solid. They are still more or less in contact. The difference is that the packing is much less orderly and that the molecular vibrations are more lively, so that the molecules can move about by exchanging sites with their neighbors more often. This is the explanation of the fact that liquids, unlike solids, can diffuse into one another. If we pour water into the lower part of a glass and carefully add a layer of a second liquid which is soluble in water (such as alcohol), then the two liquids will spontaneously intermingle without being stirred. After an interval the duration of which will depend upon the exact conditions, we shall find a homogeneous alcohol-water solution in place of the original two layers.

Gases have much lower densities than liquids or solids. When a mole of water evaporates at ordinary temperatures, its volume increases from 18 cm^3 to about 1,000 l, i.e., by about 50,000 times. The molecules are therefore much farther apart. They move around with a velocity whose average value is greater the higher the temperature and the lower the molecular weight. For molecules of molecular weight about 100 at room temperature the average velocity works out at about 2.5×10^4 cm/sec, which is about 550 miles/hr.

For most of the time a molecule in a gas is moving freely, alone and in a straight line; but at irregular intervals it will collide with another molecule, after which the two molecules will rebound from one another with altered speeds according to the laws of dynamics. The frequency of collision depends on the temperature and pressure of the gas, as well as upon the size of the molecules. If we take ordinary air as an example, each molecule experiences a collision about 10^9 times every second. This is a large number; yet a collision is over so quickly that the molecule spends most of its time between collisions, as we may see from the following considerations.

The average speed of the oxygen or nitrogen molecule in ordinary air is about 5×10^4 cm/sec. If, then, the molecule travels 5×10^4 cm each second and meantime suffers 10^9 collisions, its *mean free path* (or the average distance between collisions) works out at $(5 \times 10^4) \div 10^9 = 5 \times 10^{-5}$ cm. This is a minute enough distance by our everyday standards, but it is about a thousand times greater than a molecular diameter. A few dried peas rattling around in an otherwise empty 5-gallon keg is therefore a reasonably valid analogy for the molecules in a gas.

2

the atom

If we are to understand something about the way in which atoms join themselves together to form molecules, we must start with some ideas on atomic structure. Here we shall present briefly some of the points that seem particularly important.

Atoms vary in size according to the element, but their diameters are of the order of 1 Å (10^{-8} cm). Nearly all the mass of the atom is concentrated in its *nucleus*, with a diameter about ten thousand times smaller than that of the atom itself. The nucleus carries a positive electric charge. In terms of the natural unit of charge—that carried by the electron, e—the amount of charge carried by the nucleus is Ze, where Z is the atomic number, which is characteristic of the particular element. This number Z is also the number which falls to each element when all the elements are arranged in the natural order consistent with their properties and are then numbered off, starting with 1 for hydrogen and running up to 92 for uranium, the last of the naturally occurring elements. Table 2.1 lists the atomic numbers of the first 18 elements, which include nearly all the elements that are found in biologically important molecules. There may be several different types of nucleus with the same charge; these are called *isotopes*. For most chemical purposes they may be regarded as the same element. It is the amount of the nuclear charge that decides most of the properties of the element.

Normally, the atom is electrically neutral. The Z positive charges on the nucleus are balanced by an equal number of negatively charged electrons. These effectively occupy the remainder of the total volume of the atom. In an isolated carbon atom, for example, the nucleus, with six positive charges and over 99.9% of the mass, occupies a very small volume of about 10^{-36} cm³. The total volume of the atom is about 10^{-24} cm³, and this relatively much greater space is occupied by six electrons held by the intense

table 2.1 **electronic structure of the atoms of some of the lighter elements**

ELEMENT	ATOMIC NUMBER Z	NUMBER OF ELECTRONS IN ORBITAL OR SUBGROUP OF ORBITALS					
		$1s$	$2s$	$2p$	$3s$	$3p$	$3d$
H	1	1					
He	2	2					
Li	3	2	1	...			
Be	4	2	2	...			
B	5	2	2	1			
C	6	2	2	2			
N	7	2	2	3			
O	8	2	2	4			
F	9	2	2	5			
Ne	10	2	2	6			
Na	11	2	2	6	1	...	...
Mg	12	2	2	6	2	...	...
Al	13	2	2	6	2	1	...
Si	14	2	2	6	2	2	...
P	15	2	2	6	2	3	...
S	16	2	2	6	2	4	...
Cl	17	2	2	6	2	5	...
Ar	18	2	2	6	2	6	...

electric field of the minute nucleus. The chemical properties of the element may be largely explained by the arrangement of these electrons and the way in which they react with their environment. When this concept of atomic structure was first adopted, in about 1912, the electrons were supposed to be small particles orbiting round the nucleus in a manner similar to the movement of the earth and the other planets round the sun. This was the planetary model of the atom. The electrostatic attraction between nucleus and electron was just balanced by the centrifugal force occasioned by the movement of the electron in a circular orbit.

We now recognize that this model is unacceptable, for it is not consistent with the nature of matter on the atomic scale. Except in the very roughest approximation, the notion of electrons circling round the nucleus in definitive paths is invalid. Instead, we have to think of electron waves, or clouds of electron density, occupying the extranuclear regions of the atom. To develop these ideas in a little more detail, we shall consider the hydrogen atom. With only one electron, this is the simplest atom, and it is the only one that theory can cover at all rigorously. But the basic principles that can be discerned without too much difficulty in the theory of the hydrogen atom are also applicable in a general way to the atoms of other elements.

the hydrogen atom

Accepting the planetary model with the electron revolving in a circular orbit, the Danish physicist Niels Bohr applied the quantum theory to the hydrogen atom in 1913, and his treatment was brilliantly successful up to a point. From certain assumptions, which need not concern us, he deduced that certain orbits were possible and no others. These permissible orbits had radii which were multiples of 0.53 Å as follows: $1^2 \times 0.53$, $2^2 \times 0.53$, $3^2 \times 0.53$, etc.—that is, $n^2 \times 0.53$ Å, where n may have the integral (whole-number) values 1, 2, 3, etc. The value of n thus serves to define the orbit, and it also measures the energy of the atom: the higher n, the higher the energy. It is known as the *quantum number*.

So long as the electron stayed in a particular orbit, the energy of the atom was constant, but the energy changed abruptly if the electron jumped from one orbit to another. When the jump was to an orbit with higher n, energy was absorbed from the environment; when to one of lower n, energy was emitted, usually as light. In this way the observed frequencies of the lines in the hydrogen spectrum could be accounted for. This was the first time that any spectrum had been explained theoretically, and that it could be done with high numerical accuracy provided convincing evidence for Bohr's theory.

objections to the planetary model; wave mechanics

Nevertheless, the Bohr model had to be abandoned during the 1920's. The fundamental objection was that it contravened the *uncertainty principle*. This states that we cannot assign precise values of both position and momentum to any particle, and while the restriction is not significant for relatively large bodies of the kind we ordinarily handle, it is serious for particles as light as an electron. In other words, the laws of dynamics which work well for large objects cannot be simply applied to very small ones.

In Bohr's treatment of the planetary model, when we specify the quantum number, we imply a precisely defined radius for the electronic orbit and we also imply a precisely defined value for the energy, and hence for the momentum, too. On the atomic scale this is not possible. If, for instance, we insist on a particular amount of energy within a tolerance of $\pm 1\%$, then the uncertainty affecting the radius of the orbit becomes so large that we cannot be sure that the electron is within the atom at all.

The solution of this difficulty, and of similar difficulties affecting all atoms and molecules, lay in *wave mechanics*. Instead of regarding an electron as a small particle with a simply definable location, we have to envisage something that varies in a wavelike manner. Since waves imply some sort of vibration, the reader may well ask what is supposed to be vibrating in these electron waves. First let us consider waves of some more familiar kinds. When there are ripples on water, the surface is vibrating above and then below its normal level; when there is sound, the air pressure is vibrating between values that are alternately greater than and less than normal; when the string of, say, a violin is plucked, there is movement away from then back toward the rest position.

In electron waves the something that is vibrating is symbolized by ψ, and ψ has the property that its square, ψ^2, measures the chance of finding the electron at a particular point. The *wave function* ψ vibrates between positive and negative values on either side of zero. Since we are always directly concerned with ψ^2, we do not need to worry unduly about the fact that ψ can be negative. That it can be negative has mathematical significance, however, as we shall see later.

The wavelength λ of the waves to be associated with an electron is given by de Broglie's equation $\lambda = h/mv$.* In this equation mv stands for the momentum of the particle and, if mv is expressed in the usual gram-centimeter per second unit, h is *Planck's constant* with a numerical value of 6.6×10^{-27} erg-sec.† This equation applies to any particle, but since the constant is so small, the wavelength becomes negligibly small for ordinary objects. That is why ordinary dynamics then applies adequately.

stationary waves   Before we can understand the wave aspect of an electron in an atom or molecule, we must remind ourselves of a property characteristic of any wave motion when the waves are confined to a

---

* Count Louis Victor de Broglie, 1892—, a French physicist, received the Nobel prize for physics in 1929 for his discovery of the wave nature of the electron.

† Named for Max Planck (1852–1947), a German physicist, whose discovery that electromagnetic energy is "quantized" laid the foundation of what is now known as the quantum theory.

limited region. If a sound is made in an open space, the sound waves radiate outward and die away in the distance. By contrast, if sound is made in a closed tube, the sound wave is reflected back whenever it reaches the ends of the tube, so that very soon a set of waves is passing in either direction along the tube. Thus a system of *stationary waves* corresponding to one or other of the harmonics of the tube is established. Similarly, when a violin string is caused to vibrate by plucking, waves consisting of lateral displacement of the string travel along to the end and are reflected back. With such waves traveling both ways along the string, a system of stationary waves is again set up.

These stationary waves must be one of, or a combination of, certain discrete possibilities known as the harmonics. Some of these are represented in Fig. 2.1. The ends of the string, being fixed, are still, and there may be other points of no vibration, as in the higher harmonics, Fig. 2.1*b*, with one, and Fig. 2.1*c*, with two. Such points of no vibration are termed *nodes*. Between the nodes are regions of vibration equal in number to the number of the harmonic.

wave-mechanical theory of the hydrogen atom

When an electron is confined within the atom by the powerful electrostatic attraction of the positive nucleus, the situation resembles that in any other system of stationary waves. Like the displacement of the string, ψ can adopt one of a number of modes of vibration, or harmonics. The energy of the electron in the atom depends on the particular harmonic adopted, which turns out to be specified by a quantum number n wholly analogous to the one introduced by Bohr.

Now, the most important result of the Bohr theory for the hydrogen atom was that the energy is "quantized"; it cannot have *any*

figure 2.1

Stationary waves.

value, but only one of a number of possible values. There are certain permissible *energy levels*, and these are the fundamental realities of the situation. Instead of relating these levels, as Bohr did, to certain permitted orbits for the electron, wave mechanics relates them to certain harmonics, which are the only possible modes of the stationary electron waves when the electron is constrained to remain under the influence of the nucleus.

Here is a good example of the dictum that a successful scientific theory, though never wholly and finally right, is never wholly wrong either. The Bohr theory accounted rather accurately for the spectrum and some other, related properties of hydrogen. In due course, Bohr's actual model of circular orbits had to be abandoned; but an essential feature, the existence of energy levels, was correct. The wave-mechanical model takes over these levels and explains them more naturally.

This is also true when subtler aspects of the hydrogen spectrum are considered. Besides n, which may now be termed the *principal quantum number*, two subsidiary quantum numbers had been found necessary for a full description of the orbit. In wave mechanics three quantum numbers in all are needed for a full description of the three-dimensional system of stationary electron waves. When the proper mathematical equation for ψ is set up for an electron near a hydrogen nucleus, three quantities appear. These three quantities must have certain integral values if the equation is to be soluble for constant energy.

For our purposes it suffices to give the rules governing the permissible values for the three quantum numbers. The principal quantum number n may, as before, have any integral value from 1 upward. The second one, the *azimuthal quantum number l*, may have any positive, integral value less than n, but including zero. The third one, the *magnetic quantum number m*, may have any positive or negative integral value, including zero, from $+l$ to $-l$. The possibilities, for values of n up to 3, are given in Table 2.2.

orbitals Instead of the word "orbit," which was appropriate to the Bohr model, wave mechanics generally uses *orbital*. It corresponds formally to a possible set of the three quantum numbers, and it may be envisaged as a possible harmonic, or mode of vibration,

table 2.2 **possible atomic orbitals**

n	1	2		3		
l	0	0	1	0	1	2
m	0	0	$-1,\ 0,\ +1$	0	$-1,\ 0,\ +1$	$-2,\ -1, 0, +1, +2$
Number of orbitals	1	1	3	1	3	5
Total orbitals	1	4		9		
Symbol	$1s$	$2s$	$2p$	$3s$	$3p$	$3d$

of the stationary electron waves in the atom. An isolated hydrogen atom must necessarily have its electron in one of these orbitals. Probably it will be in one of those shown in the table; although if the atom has been *excited* by absorption of an unusually large amount of energy, the orbital may be one with a higher value of n.

A particular atomic orbital is usually symbolized by the number for n and by an italic letter denoting the value of l. This letter is given by the following code: s for $l = 0$, p for $l = 1$, d for $l = 2$, and f for $l = 3$. (There is a reason in the history of spectroscopy for these seemingly arbitrarily chosen letters; they stand for the sharp, principal, diffuse, and fundamental series of spectral lines. But we need not concern ourselves with this, nor with the continuation of the code for higher values of l, which hardly ever enter into chemical considerations anyway.) The orbital symbols thus derived are given in the bottom row of Table 2.2.

The reader may ask why we have not mentioned a symbol to specify the value of the third quantum number m. This is unnecessary, because a set of orbitals differing only in their values of m are, for most purposes, indistinguishable. All the same, it is important to remember that there may be several orbitals within the subgroup: one s orbital, but three p and five d orbitals. These numbers are listed in the fourth row of Table 2.2, while the fifth row shows the total number of orbitals with each value of n. These totals are in fact always equal to n^2, and it is not difficult to demonstrate mathematically that this follows from the rules given above.

The level of lowest energy is known as the *ground state*. This is the situation in which an atom or molecule normally exists, though it may sometimes get excited to a higher level. The hydrogen atom in its ground state has its single electron in the 1s orbital. This fact is recorded in Table 2.1.

atoms with more than one electron

In elements other than hydrogen the atom has more than one electron. This complicates the situation. A rigorous solution is difficult when there are two electrons; it is impossible when there are more than two. (This should not cause us undue dejection; for the dynamical problem of three bodies has so far resisted solution. The astronomers can compute the orbit of the moon, traveling under the combined attractions of earth and sun, with great accuracy. But they must do so by a complex process of successive approximation, and not by the clean solution of the basic equations of motion.) Nevertheless, the general system of orbitals described for the hydrogen atom carries over to many-electron atoms. This affords an invaluable, if qualitative, understanding of their electronic arrangements. Two principles are essential for this extension.

1. The same sets of orbitals are available, and they may be given the same designations: 1s, 2s, 2p, 3s, etc. In an element of higher atomic number, however, they will be drawn more closely in toward the nucleus because of the greater attraction exerted by the multiple positive charge. Consequently, the electron in any orbital will be more firmly held—or be harder to remove—than a corresponding electron in hydrogen would be. This "tightening up" is not simple, because the other electrons tend to offset partially the enhanced attraction of the nucleus.

2. Any one orbital can never accommodate more than two electrons. This arises from the *Pauli principle*, formulated by the Austrian-born physicist Wolfgang Pauli (1900–1958), and the phenomenon of *electron spin*, both of which we must briefly explain. An electron possesses a magnetic moment; it acts as if it were a small magnet with north and south poles. This would be the result if the electron, regarded for this purpose as a negatively charged sphere, were rotating about an axis.

That such a spinning of the electron should be taken literally is doubtful, but the magnetic moment is certain enough. A magnet placed in a magnetic field will tend to orient itself so that its poles lie along the direction of the field. The electron has an analogous tendency, though, in accordance with quantum principles, there are two possible orientations for the electron. These need to be specified by a quantum number, the *electron-spin quantum number* s, which can have two values only: $+\frac{1}{2}$ and $-\frac{1}{2}$, corresponding to the two possible orientations. These values are numerically equal and differ by 1. (This use of the symbol s should not be confused with the use to denote an orbital with $l = 0$.)

From all this it follows that altogether *four* quantum numbers are required to specify the situation of an electron in an atom: n, l, and m for the orbital and s for the spin. A simple form of the Pauli principle is that no two electrons in the same atom may have the same values of all four quantum numbers. In other words, when n, l, and m have been stated, thereby defining the orbital, s must be either $+\frac{1}{2}$ or $-\frac{1}{2}$. The orbital can accommodate only two electrons, and they must have opposite spins.

atomic structure and the periodic table

We can now develop the electronic structures of the first few elements in the periodic table. These structures are shown in Table 2.1, in all cases for the atom in its ground state. The electrons go first into the orbital of lowest energy ($1s$); when this is full with a pair of electrons possessing opposite spins, the third and fourth electrons go into the next lowest orbital ($2s$); and so on. The order of the orbitals shown in Table 2.2 is also the order of increasing energy of their electrons. (Strictly, this is true only for the first five orbitals listed. With higher orbitals some complications occur, but they do not affect the lighter elements.)

When the first *shell* with $n = 1$ (and the single $1s$ orbital) is just filled, we have an especially stable arrangement of electrons corresponding to the chemical inertness of helium. When the second shell with $n = 2$ (and four $2s$ or $2p$ orbitals) is just filled, we have another very stable arrangement in another inert gas, neon. Since this shell accommodates eight electrons, we sometimes say that the octet has been completed. Over the next eight elements, sodium to argon, another octet is completed with eight electrons in the four $3s$ and $3p$ orbitals. Although the shell with $n = 3$ is still incomplete, the five $3d$ orbitals still being vacant, the arrangement is again remarkably stable. Argon is another inert gas.

The electronic structures shown in Table 2.1 are easy to remember. Certainly the reader should memorize those for hydrogen, carbon, nitrogen, oxygen, phosphorus, and sulfur; for it is of these elements that biologically important molecules are mainly composed. We may reiterate these structures and, at the same time, introduce a convenient way to represent them: H, $1s^1$; C, $1s^22s^22p^2$; N, $1s^22s^22p^3$; O, $1s^22s^22p^4$; P, $1s^22s^22p^63s^23p^3$; and S, $1s^22s^22p^63s^23p^4$. The superscript numbers give the total of the electrons in the group of orbitals covered.

the shapes of orbitals

One further property of atomic orbitals is essential for our understanding of molecule building. This concerns their shapes. We start with the simpler case of the shapes of the stationary waves for the vibrating string, illustrated in Fig. 2.1. If n here stands for the harmonic, this is wholly analogous to the principal quantum number for the electron. In each harmonic of the string there are $n - 1$ nodes, in addition to the points of no vibration at the ends. The stretched string is a one-dimensional vibrator, and for it the nodes are *points*. The electron waves in an atom are three-dimensional, which is more difficult to draw on paper or to envisage; but we can state that the nodes are two-dimensional—there are *nodal surfaces*.

There is another difference. The electron waves around an atom do not cease abruptly at the outer edge, as do the vibrations of the string. Rather, they die away gradually. We cannot regard the atom as having a sharply demarked boundary. However, the fall-off of electron density is fairly sharp. Taking hydrogen as an example, the chance of finding an electron at, say, 0.8 Å from the nucleus would be reasonably high, whereas at 1.1 Å it would be very much less. So to regard the hydrogen atom as having an effective radius of about 1.0 Å is a useful, rough approximation.

With this understanding we may now describe the shapes of the stationary-wave systems for s and p orbitals. All s orbitals are spherically symmetrical; they die away similarly in all directions. For the simplest s orbital ($1s$) we can think of the electron density as a fuzzy ball with ψ (and hence ψ^2 too) high near the central

figure 2.2

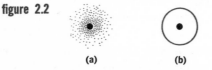

(a)   (b)

Representations of an s orbital.

figure 2.3

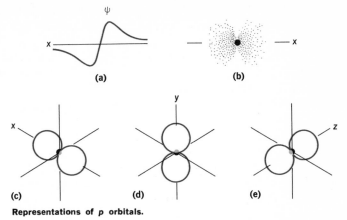

Representations of p orbitals.

nucleus and diminishing outward, as suggested by Fig. 2.2a. Much more conventionally, this can also be suggested by Fig. 2.2b, a form of diagram which is much easier to draw.

Any p orbital has a nodal plane passing through the nucleus. On this plane ψ is zero. In Fig. 2.3a we represent the variation of ψ along a line through the nucleus and perpendicular to the nodal plane. That ψ is shown to be negative at one side is incidental only, since it is ψ^2 that represents the electron density. This density must therefore be zero on the nodal plane, increase on either side at first, and then gradually die away. We may therefore follow the conventions of Fig. 2.2 and represent the p orbital by Fig. 2.3b or c, the former being rather more exact in the impression it gives, and the latter much easier to draw.

For any given value of n there are three possible p orbitals. They arise because there are three independent ways to orient the nodal plane; so that the extension of electron density sketched in Fig. 2.3c may be in any of three mutually perpendicular directions. Remembering the axes of coordinate geometry, we may label these directions x, y, and z. So if the orbital of Fig. 2.3 is denoted by p_x, with the lobes of electron density to right and left, the p_y and p_z orbitals might be represented by Fig. 2.3d and e, with the lobes respectively above and below and in front and behind. All three orbitals are equivalent; which label we attach to which is arbitrary.

3

valence and its electronic interpretation

On page 7 we mentioned the development of the notion of valence: that each atom of any particular element possesses a certain number of units of combining power toward other atoms. We now wish to consider this notion in rather more detail.

Valence is usually shown in its simplest form when an element combines with hydrogen, because hydrogen itself is normally univalent. Considering the elements carbon, nitrogen, oxygen, and fluorine, we notice that their simplest compounds with hydrogen have molecules with the formulas CH_4, NH_3, OH_2, and FH. Carbon is quadrivalent, and it can form four bonds, one to each hydrogen atom. Similarly, nitrogen can form three bonds, oxygen two, and fluorine one. These numbers can be maintained in nearly all compounds of these respective elements, as we illustrated in some of the formulas of Chap. 1. Once established, such rules were of great value in constructing formulas for other molecules. For instance, each carbon atom in any formula must have four bonds linking it to other atoms. To maintain this rule, double bonds, as in $O{=}C{=}O$ (carbon dioxide) and $H_2C{=}CH_2$ (ethylene), or triple bonds, as in $HC{\equiv}CH$ (acetylene), are sometimes necessary. Given this possibility, there are almost no exceptions so far as the atoms C, N, and O are concerned.

This concept of valence as a number worked extremely well in organic chemistry and was firmly established by 1900, but in that "classical period" there could be no theory of how valence operated *as a force*. The lack of any knowledge of atomic structure precluded any useful speculation about the manner in which atoms combined. With the discovery of the electron and the recognition that it is a universal constituent of matter, the situation began to change. But a serviceable theory of valence had to wait until a sound idea of atomic structure had been established in 1912. In fact, the first generally acceptable theories were suggested in 1916 by Walter Kossel, in Germany, and more particularly by G. N. Lewis, in the United States. Though acceptable, there was some delay before these ideas were adopted by the majority of chemists. The publication of three celebrated papers by the American chemist Irving Langmuir, in 1919–1920, and of a book entitled "The Electronic Theory of Valency" by the English chemist Nevil Vincent Sidgwick (1873–1952), in 1927, may be taken to mark the beginning and end of this phase.

Toward the end of this period there began the further task of interpreting the mechanism of valence in more detail with the aid of wave mechanics, and this work still occupies theoretical chemists. However, we need not yet concern ourselves with this more difficult aspect. We shall first concentrate on the earlier electronic theory, which we may regard as a set of rules for writing formulas for molecules with a proper understanding, at the simplest level, of their electronic implications.

the electronic interpretation of electrovalence

We start with two propositions: (1) that there are certain groupings of electrons, around an atomic nucleus, which are peculiarly stable and (2) that an atom which does not initially possess the number of electrons corresponding to one of these favored groupings tends to gain, or lose, electrons so as to attain that number. Very often, though not always, the number of electrons conferring stability on an atom is that occurring in the nearest inert gas. For the first score of elements this is nearly always so, and for that reason Table 2.1 is important to us.

Especially stable groupings shown in the table are the ones in helium (two electrons), neon (10), and argon (18). These elements are unreactive because their atoms already have these numbers of electrons arranged as given in the table. The atom of sodium, by contrast, has 11 electrons—$1s^2 \ 2s^2 \ 2p^6 \ 3s^1$—one more than neon. Hence the sodium atom readily loses its outermost ($3s$) electron. It thereby acquires a single net positive charge, since the nuclear charge of $+11$ units is now counterbalanced by only 10 negative electrons. It is said to have become an *ion*, which we represent as Na^+. On the other hand, a fluorine atom has 9 electrons—$1s^2 \ 2s^2 \ 2p^5$—one less than neon. So it is ready to acquire an electron to fill the $2p$ orbitals and to complete the octet; $2s^2$,

$2p^6$. By so doing, it comes to possess a net negative charge since the nuclear charge of $+9$ is now overcompensated by 10 negative electrons. It is said to have become a fluoride *ion*, represented as F^-.

The outcome of this transfer of electrons from sodium to fluorine atoms is the production of equal numbers of positively and negatively charged ions. The electrostatic attraction between ions of opposite charge is the immediate explanation of the chemical combination represented by the familiar chemical equation, $2Na + F_2 \rightarrow 2NaF$. Valence arising in this way is known as *electrovalence*. Sodium fluoride is known as an *ionic compound*.

How these oppositely charged ions arrange themselves depends on the conditions. Ordinarily, sodium fluoride, like other salts, is a crystalline solid. Its crystal structure, which is sketched in Fig. 3.1, is identical with that of sodium chloride. This diagram corresponds to only a single unit of the structure. The pattern must be supposed to extend in all directions to the limits of the actual crystal. On the scale of this diagram the extension is virtually infinite: a crystal of dimensions 1 mm each way, for instance, would have the motif shown in Fig. 3.1 repeated about five million times in each direction. Every sodium ion has, as nearest neighbors, six equidistant fluoride ions; every fluoride has six equidistant sodium ions. An important feature of this

figure 3.1

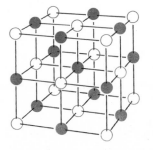

The arrangement of ions in the crystal of sodium fluoride and of other substances with the rock salt structure. The shaded circles represent one type of ion—either Na^+ or F^-—and the open circles the other type.

structure is that no discrete sodium fluoride *molecule* can be identified in it. The same is true of all salts, even if their crystal structures are much more complicated.

When this situation was first discovered, in about 1913, most chemists were surprised. As we suggested in Chap. 1, the notion of the molecule had proved invaluable, especially in organic chemistry and for simple inorganic gases. Salts were thought of as having similar molecules: univalent sodium and fluorine were supposed to form an Na—F molecule. So far as solid salts are concerned, this idea has had to be abandoned. Each ion of one kind has several similarly positioned neighbors of the other kind; we cannot justly pick on any particular pair as constituting a molecule.

There is the same absence of recognizable molecules in solution. A salt dissolved in water consists almost wholly of ions. A small fraction of a percent of the ions may, at any instant, exist as transient *ion pairs* (Na^+F^-), but generally there is no molecule.

A more detailed consideration of electrovalence is possible if we adopt a type of formula that shows the outer electrons of each atom. The usual convention is to represent an electron by a dot, and we slightly change the meaning of the chemical symbol so that it signifies the "core" or "kernel" of the atom only—all the atom except the outermost shell of electrons. The transference of an electron between sodium and fluorine atoms is then portrayed as follows:

$$\cdot Na + \cdot \overset{\cdot\cdot}{\underset{\cdot\cdot}{F}} : \; \rightarrow \; Na^+ + : \overset{\cdot\cdot}{\underset{\cdot\cdot}{F}} : ^-$$

Other examples may be taken from the formation of magnesium chloride $MgCl_2$ and calcium oxide CaO:

$$: Mg + 2 \cdot \overset{\cdot\cdot}{\underset{\cdot\cdot}{Cl}} : \; \rightarrow \; Mg^{++} + 2 : \overset{\cdot\cdot}{\underset{\cdot\cdot}{Cl}} : ^-$$

$$: Ca + \quad \overset{\cdot\cdot}{\underset{\cdot\cdot}{O}} : \; \rightarrow \; Ca^{++} + \quad : \overset{\cdot\cdot}{\underset{\cdot\cdot}{O}} : ^-$$

At first sight the reader might expect a wide variety of ionic combination by electrovalence. For instance, we have just represented a magnesium atom losing two electrons to yield an ion with a neon-like structure, Mg^{++} $1s^2$ $2s^2$ $2p^6$. If this atom were to gain six electrons, it would attain an argon-like structure, Mg^{6-} $1s^2$ $2s^2$ $2p^6$ $3s^2$ $3p^6$, with 18 electrons. Conversely, the chlorine atom might lose seven electrons to attain a neon-like structure, Cl^{7+} $1s^2$ $2s^2$ $2p^6$, instead of gaining one electron to become argon-like as was implied above. In fact, there is a severe limitation on the numbers of electrons that can be gained or lost in this way.

Ions with multiple charges are uncommon. Negative ions rarely, if ever, carry more than two charges; positive ions may occasionally have three charges, or even four, but not more. To remove seven electrons from chlorine, to produce Cl^{7+}, would require too much energy. The high negative charge on a hypothetical Mg^{6-} ion would render it too unstable; the mutual repulsion of several more electrons than correspond to the positive charges on the nucleus would cause the ion to "fly apart." All the commonly occurring ions are produced by the gain or loss of one, two, or at most three electrons.

covalence and molecules

The concept of electrovalence can explain chemical combination in certain types of compounds, notably salts. But these are compounds in which a molecule proves not to be an obvious feature of the situation, as we now understand it. Substances with well-characterized molecules, such as H_2, H_2O, CO_2, CH_4, and nearly all organic compounds, do not have the properties of salts, and they cannot be sensibly represented as being electrovalent.

Let us try to represent the carbon dioxide molecule in this way. We can formally postulate that the carbon atom loses four electrons, two to each of the oxygens. The carbon is thereby left with a helium-like number of electrons and a quadruple positive ionic charge, and each oxygen assumes a neon-like number with a double negative ionic charge:

$$\overset{\cdot}{\underset{\cdot}{\cdot\text{C}\cdot}} + 2\ \overset{\cdot\cdot}{\underset{\cdot\cdot}{\text{O}}}\text{:} \rightarrow C^{4+} + 2\ \overset{\cdot\cdot}{\underset{\cdot\cdot}{\text{:O:}}}^{=}$$

Apart from the objection to multiply charged ions, this is unconvincing, since carbon dioxide is not an ionic compound. Unlike any salt, it is a gas at ordinary temperatures, and it certainly does not give carbon or oxide ions in solution. Still less plausible would be an attempt to portray H_2 or CH_4 as an electrovalent substance.

We are thus led to recognize a rough, but general, division of chemical substances into two types: the salts, which can be reasonably regarded as ionic and whose formation can be attributed to electrovalence, and others, with recognizable molecules, which need some other explanation for the forces holding their atoms together.

A clue, if not a full explanation, was first given by Lewis in 1916. He suggested an alternative method by which an atom might achieve a stable electronic grouping: by *sharing pairs of electrons*. With the shared pair, counting toward each of the two atoms at the same time, each atom could rate as having the number of electrons necessary for stability. The hydrogen molecule is the simplest example. Each hydrogen atom initially has one electron, but it requires two to become helium-like. If a pair of atoms can share electrons, each atom will achieve stability:

$$H^{\cdot} + {\cdot}H \rightarrow H:H$$

In methane, CH_4, the hydrogen atoms acquire similar helium-like pairs, while the carbon completes an octet and becomes neon-like:

$$4H^{\cdot} + {\cdot}\overset{\cdot\cdot}{\underset{\cdot}{C}}{\cdot} \rightarrow H:\overset{\overset{\textstyle H}{\cdot\cdot}}{\underset{\underset{\textstyle \ddot{H}}{\cdot\cdot}}{C}}:H$$

In carbon dioxide all three atoms achieve octets:

$$2\,\overset{\cdot\cdot}{\underset{\cdot\cdot}{O}}: + {\cdot}\overset{\cdot}{\underset{\cdot}{C}}{\cdot} \rightarrow :\overset{\cdot}{O}::C::\overset{\cdot}{\underset{\cdot}{O}}:$$

(We shall see later that this last formula can be improved by a more sophisticated treatment.) *Covalence* was the name given by Langmuir to this type of bonding by shared electron pairs.

bond diagrams, their construction and uses

When electronic formulas are compared with the classical formulas appearing on page 7, we notice that a bond of the latter is now consistently represented by two dots signifying a shared pair. This is always true so long as we are dealing with covalences. Therefore, we can now adopt this as a valuable convention and allow the use of the line, or bond, for shared electron pairs. A formula, or a *bond diagram*, like O=C=O thus takes on a new significance.

Indeed, we can go a little further and allow the line to stand also for an unshared pair of electrons when we wish to emphasize its presence in a molecule. We can illustrate this possibility by setting out in some detail the electronic formulation of the molecules of water and ammonia. We must begin by totaling the number of valence electrons for which we have to account. In both of these molecules there are eight: initially, six in the outer shell of the oxygen atom and one on each of the two hydrogens, and five on nitrogen and one on each of three hydrogens, respectively. The electronic formulas must then be

$$\begin{array}{ccc} \text{H}-\overline{\text{O}}\text{I} & \text{and} & \text{H}-\overline{\text{N}}-\text{H} \\ | & & | \\ \text{H} & & \text{H} \end{array}$$

They may be written in an alternative convention:

$$\begin{array}{cc} \text{H}-\overset{..}{\text{O}}: & \text{H}-\overset{..}{\text{N}}-\text{H} \\ | & | \\ \text{H} & \text{H} \end{array}$$

We check the number of valence electrons appearing and duly find the correct number, eight, in each case. Sometimes we do not trouble to show the unshared pairs, and then these formulas reduce to

$$\begin{array}{cc} \text{H}-\text{O} & \text{H}-\text{N}-\text{H} \\ | & | \\ \text{H} & \text{H} \end{array}$$

but the other electrons are then *understood* to be present. In fact, the presence on an atom of these unshared electron pairs often accounts for special properties in the molecule. Their importance justifies the use of a special name: they are usually known, picturesquely, as *lone pairs*.

The reader should acquire a facility in working out electronic formulas for simple covalent molecules. As examples, we suggest ethylene, C_2H_4; acetic acid, CH_3COOH; ethyl alcohol, C_2H_5OH;

acetone, CH_3COCH_3; and carbon monoxide, CO, which will be found to have the following bond diagrams:

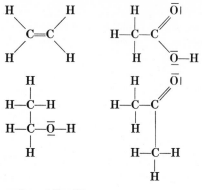

and $|C\equiv O|$

dative covalence

In the electronic formulas we have so far discussed, the covalent bond has been produced by each atom providing one electron toward the shared pair. In general, we can suppose the bond to have been formed thus:

$$A^{\cdot} + {\cdot}B \rightarrow A:B$$

only the bonding electrons being shown. This constitutes a *normal covalent bond*. Sometimes, however, one atom provides both electrons in a manner we can formally represent thus:

$$D: + E \rightarrow D:E$$

This bond is still covalent, but we may wish to call attention to the difference in its method of formation. If we do, we call the bond a *dative covalence* or a *coordinate bond*. One reason why we may wish to emphasize the distinction is that a dative bond, when formed between initially uncharged atoms, leads to a net separation of positive and negative charge. This may be demonstrated by the following argument. If D and E are electrically neutral, we may imagine that one electron is first transferred to E. Just as in an electrovalent transaction, this produces two ions:

$$D: + E \rightarrow D^{\cdot +} + {\cdot}E^{-}$$

Each atom now has an electron to contribute toward the covalent bond, but the ionic charges would remain:

$$D^{\cdot +} + {\cdot}E^{-} \rightarrow \overset{+}{D}:\overset{-}{E} \text{ or } \overset{+}{D}{-}\overset{-}{E}$$

In a sense, this bond is both an electrovalence and a covalence. We may then contrast the normal bond in A—B with the dative one in $\overset{+}{D}$—$\overset{-}{E}$. The positive and negative charges in the latter formula are known as *formal charges*. The adjective reminds us that this is a rough-and-ready representation. There will be some tendency toward a separation of charges in the DE molecule, but we do not really know whether it amounts to a full unit of charge, nor do we know the exact location of the positive and negative parts of it.

As an example, we consider the molecule of an amine oxide. The three hydrogen atoms in ammonia may be replaced by methyl groups, CH_3, giving trimethylamine, $(CH_3)_3N$. The reader should check the electronic formula given below and note the lone pair on the nitrogen atom. This molecule can combine with an oxygen atom to yield trimethylamine oxide:

$$CH_3\!-\!\underset{\underset{\displaystyle CH_3}{|}}{\overset{\overset{\displaystyle CH_3}{|}}{N}}| \quad + \quad \overset{-}{O}| \quad \rightarrow \quad CH_3\!-\!\underset{\underset{\displaystyle CH_3}{|}}{\overset{\overset{\displaystyle CH_3}{|}}{\overset{\oplus}{N}}}\!-\!\overset{-}{O}|\ominus$$

The formal charges, which we have ringed to avoid possible confusion between the minus sign and the unshared pairs, indicate that the N—O bond is dative.

Occasionally the dative character of a covalent bond is signified in another way. Instead of with formal charges, the bond is marked with an arrow pointing in the direction in which the lone pair was donated. Thus an alternative formula for trimethylamine oxide would be

$$CH_3\!-\!\underset{\underset{\displaystyle CH_3}{|}}{\overset{\overset{\displaystyle CH_3}{|}}{N}}\!\rightarrow\!O$$

The nitrogen and oxygen atoms before union carried no charge, and this is essential for the formation of an unambiguous dative bond. We can illustrate this point by a contrary example which is also instructive in other ways: the formation of an ammonium salt. When ammonia is mixed with a solution of an acid, an ammonium salt is formed; with hydrochloric acid, for instance, it gives ammonium chloride, NH_4^+ Cl^-. The role of the acid is to provide a hydrogen ion or, essentially, a proton, and the material act is the union of the proton with the lone pair of the nitrogen atom:

$$
\begin{array}{c}
\text{H} \\
| \\
\text{H}-\text{N}| \\
| \\
\text{H}
\end{array}
+ \text{H}^+ \rightarrow
\left[
\begin{array}{c}
\text{H} \\
| \\
\text{H}-\text{N}-\text{H} \\
| \\
\text{H}
\end{array}
\right]^+
$$

Both the electrons are provided by the nitrogen atom, so that at first sight we might take the new N—H bond to be dative. Then we realize that, once formed, all four bonds are equivalent; we cannot reasonably take one of them to be dative and the other three to be normal covalences. In this situation we just refuse to answer the apparently straight question, "Is this bond normal or dative?" with a plain yes or no. The important points are that all the bonds are covalent and equivalent and that the entity is a singly charged positive ion which we represent in the usual way without committing ourselves as to the precise location of the charge.

The dative bond occurs in *coordination compounds* of metals. Classical examples are the various cobaltammines, which are based on the salts of trivalent cobalt such as Co^{3+} $3Cl^-$. Six ammonia molecules may each donate a lone pair of electrons to build a group of 12 electrons around the cobalt atom, forming the complex ion $[Co(NH_3)_6]^{3+}$, which may be formulated as in (1). The ammonia molecules are said to be *coordinated* to the cobalt ion. Various other entities which are capable of donating a lone pair may behave similarly, a water molecule being one example.

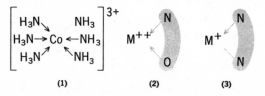

(1)   (2)   (3)

It sometimes happens that two or more of the coordinating groups belong to the same molecule, as shown schematically in (2), or one group may be attached to the central ion by a normal covalent bond and the other by a dative one (3). Coordination compounds of this closed-ring type are known as *chelates*, and many important examples occur in biological systems. Four nitrogen atoms belonging to the same large molecule are chelated to the iron atom to constitute the heme group in hemoglobin, and a similar structure occurs around the magnesium atom in a molecule of chlorophyll.

the theory of the covalent bond

There is no difficulty in recognizing the cause of the chemical union in the case of electrovalent compounds. The oppositely charged ions (e.g., Na^+ and Cl^-) attract one another, and this type of electrostatic force—the *Coulomb force* it is sometimes called, after the French physicist Charles Augustin de Coulomb—has been known to physics for two centuries or more. It is therefore familiar and seems to present no mystery, though it would be unwise to pretend that we really *understand* the force.

Covalence is much harder to explain. Classical physics gives no reason why two atoms should share a pair of electrons or why this sharing, whatever that means, should give rise to a force of attraction just about as strong as that between two ions. It is therefore important that wave mechanics (see pages 21 to 29) has given us some understanding of covalence.

We must now face the task of sketching the theory of the covalent bond. The task is difficult for two reasons. First, the argument is mathematical, and we do not wish to assume that all readers of this book are mathematically well equipped. Second, even for those who are fairly well equipped, the mathematics is hard. Even the simplest ordinary molecule, H_2, embodies four particles—two nuclei and two electrons; and such a problem is not rigorously soluble in classical dynamics, nor is it in wave mechanics. By assuming that the heavier nuclei remain stationary, some alleviation is possible, but to do accurate calculations is still a formidable task. With a molecule such as CH_4, which has 10 electrons, accurate calculations are impracticable; with benzene, possessing 30 valence electrons, still more so.

Nevertheless, our being able to "explain" the bonding in H_2 by calculating certain properties of that molecule and obtaining results in good agreement with experiment gives us some general understanding of other valence bonds. Furthermore, by approximate methods, we can obtain useful results for more complicated molecules, and these increase our feeling of comprehension.

We shall consider the hydrogen molecule first, and in some detail. We shall try to convey an impression of how the atoms are held together, but without giving the mathematics necessary for a thorough understanding. In Fig. 3.2a we sketch a situation in which the two electrons occupy positions between the two positively charged nuclei. To be sure, the uncertainty principle (page 21) forbids us to envisage the electrons as definitely located at two particular points; but we have shaded an area between the nuclei, and it is permissible to suppose that the chance of finding both electrons in this region is relatively high and that it is relatively low elsewhere. If this electron distribution occurs, there will certainly be an attractive force between the nuclei, since each nucleus is attracted by the electron cloud and this attraction will outweigh the repulsion between the nuclei, which are farther apart.

Given the situation shown in Fig. 3.2, we can understand how an attraction arises by an electrostatic effect. What is hard to understand is why the electrons should behave in this way. Two negatively charged particles normally repel one another. It is because of their wave nature that the electrons may, in certain circumstances, crowd into a region where classical theory would not lead us to expect them. This is the basic fact that makes the application of wave mechanics to valence problems important.

In an atom the electron occupies an *atomic orbital*, or AO. The AO is represented by a particular wave function ψ, which has different values at different points around the nucleus such that

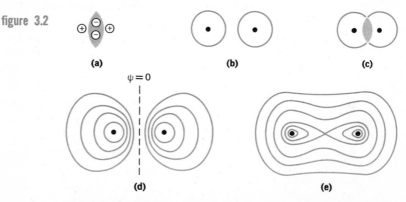

figure 3.2

Formation of a hydrogen molecule from two atoms. In *(d)* and *(e)* electron density is represented by contour lines, the zero contour in *(d)* being shown as a broken line.

ψ^2 gives the probability of finding the electron at any given point, as was explained on page 22. The AO can be regarded as a possible set of stationary electron waves. One orbital can contain not more than two electrons, which must have opposite spins. In a molecule the electrons—or at any rate those that are involved in bonding—occupy *molecular orbitals*, or MO's. An MO is a more complicated function which extends over the region around two or more atomic nuclei; it represents a possible set of stationary electron waves when the electron is under the control of several nuclei. One way to envisage how MO's might arise is to suppose them to be formed by combining AO's.

For the H_2 molecule we start with two isolated hydrogen atoms, each in its ground state of lowest energy. As we saw on page 27, the electron is in a $1s$ orbital, which is spherically symmetrical as represented in Fig. 2.2. We show two neighboring, but unconnected, atoms by this convention in Fig. 3.2*b*. The $1s$ orbital has no nodes, resembling the first harmonic of a vibrating string shown in Fig. 2.1, and ψ can be regarded as vibrating between positive and negative values. (The positive and negative values of ψ must not be confused with the positive and negative electrical charges of nucleus and electron.)

As we have already emphasized, the $+$ or $-$ has no direct physical significance, since it is ψ^2 that measures the electron density. However, the sign of ψ does become significant when we form an MO by allowing two AO's to overlap. An overlap occurs when the two atoms approach one another, as is signified in Fig. 3.2*c*. There are, in fact, two basically different ways in which the overlap can take place: (1) The wave functions can be in phase, so that, when ψ for one atom is $+$, so also is ψ for the other. (2) They can be out of phase, so that ψ is $+$ for one atom when ψ for the other is $-$. The latter mode of interaction is suggested in Fig. 3.2*d*, where electron density is indicated by contours. It leads to a nodal plane, with $\psi = 0$, midway between the nuclei; for this plane is the locus of points that are equidistant from each nucleus and the ψ's, since they are exactly equivalent but of opposite sign, must cancel each other at all points on this plane. This means that ψ^2, the electron density, is also zero.

In other words, the electrons avoid the region between the nuclei when they are in an MO formed by an out-of-phase combination of the AO's. On the other hand, when a combination is in phase, the MO gives a relatively high electron density between the nuclei and an attractive force results. Detailed calculations can be made, and their outcome is suggested by the contour lines of Fig. 3.2d and e. The favorable MO represented by Fig. 3.2e is said to be *bonding*, while that of Fig. 3.2d is *antibonding*.

We may recapitulate as follows:

1. According to wave mechanics, electrons are represented by wave functions ψ such that ψ^2 at any point measures the chance of finding an electron there.

2. In an atom the electrons are confined in the region around the nucleus and are represented by stationary waves any particular node of which, known as an atomic orbital, may contain not more than a pair of electrons.

3. In a molecule the electrons concerned in valence are in molecular orbitals, which can be represented as stationary-wave systems involving more than one nucleus.

4. Certain of these molecular orbitals require that there be a relatively high chance of finding both electrons of the orbital in the region between the atomic nuclei. These are bonding MO's; they correspond to low energy and hence to a stable molecule. The pair of electrons in such an MO acts as a "negative cement" holding the positive nuclei together.

the molecular-orbital approximation
We have already explained that a rigorous treatment of any molecule more complicated than H_2 is mathematically too difficult. Approximate methods have to be used. Two such methods have proved particularly helpful both in giving us some insight into the valence problem and also in enabling us to calculate certain properties of molecules. These are the *molecular-orbital* (MO) and *valence-bond* (VB) methods. The latter we shall discuss in the next section. The former we have already used in our elementary consideration of the hydrogen molecule. We now apply it to some more complicated, but still very simple, molecules. Though quantitative calculations can be made with the MO approximation, we shall confine ourselves to using it in a descriptive and qualitative way.

The basic notion is that an MO is likely to be formed more effectively the more the AO's overlap with each other. With *s* orbitals, which extend similarly in all directions, there is no particular direction of most favorable overlap. But p and d orbitals have more complicated shapes (page 29), so that optimal overlap depends critically on direction.

The water molecule illustrates the method well. We start with the three atoms in their ground states, and we look out especially for their unpaired electrons. Each hydrogen atom is in its $1s$ state, with its single, unpaired electron occupying the spherically symmetrical AO. The oxygen atom has the electronic structure $1s^2$ $2s^2$ $2p^4$. We are concerned here only with the four p electrons, whose arrangement among the three orbitals is often represented as , where the arrows indicate the relative directions of the electron spins. The three p orbitals extend in three mutually perpendicular directions. We may arbitrarily suppose the first orbital, with its full complement of electrons, to lie in the z direction. It is the remaining two, p_x and p_y, each with its single electron, that interest us particularly. Concentrating attention on the four unpaired electrons, we may represent the initial situation of the three atoms by Fig. 3.3a. Overlap of the hydrogen AO's, each with a p orbital of the oxygen atom, can take place if the hydrogen atoms approach the oxygen along the x and y directions, as shown in Fig. 3.3b. The overlap in these positions leads to the formation of MO's, one bonding and the other antibonding in each case. For an attractive force we are concerned only with the bonding orbitals, and these can be represented by the shapes drawn in Fig. 3.3c. Two MO's have been formed, approximately at right angles to each other, and in them the four valence electrons can be accommodated with a diminution of total energy and hence with stabilization of the water molecule.

figure 3.3

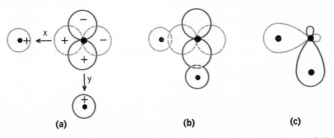

(a) (b) (c)

Formation of a water molecule by overlapping of the s orbitals of the hydrogen atoms each with a p orbital of the oxygen atom.

At one time it must have seemed likely that the water molecule would have its three atoms in line: H—O—H. As we shall describe in Chap. 4, we now have plenty of evidence that it is bent, rather than linear, the two hydrogens subtending an angle of rather more than 100° at the oxygen atom. This fact, which is of the greatest importance as we shall see on pages 129 to 139, is easily explained by the MO theory: A pair of p orbitals are involved, and they lie at 90° to one another. Some repulsion between the two sets of bonding electrons accounts for the angle being rather more than 90° in the actual molecule.

The reader should work out for himself the similar MO interpretation of the ammonia molecule and thus arrive at an explanation of the fact that this molecule has a pyramidal shape with its three hydrogen atoms at the corners of an equilateral triangle and the nitrogen at the apex of a pyramid based on the triangle.

the hybridization of atomic orbitals

When we try to apply the MO method to carbon compounds, we run into difficulties. Let us try to formulate the methane, CH_4, molecule. Besides the four hydrogens, we start with a carbon atom in its ground state, which has the structure $1s^2\ 2s^2\ 2p^2$. The p orbitals are represented by the diagram ⌈↑│↑│ ⌉. There are only two unpaired electrons. Following the argument given above, we should suppose the carbon to be capable of forming bonds with only two hydrogen atoms. The valence can be raised to 4 by "promoting" one electron from the $2s$ to the $2p$ orbital, which yields the structure $1s^2\ 2s^1\ 2p^3$, with four unpaired spins. But this would lead to unequal bonding. There would be a good overlap between the s orbital of each of the three hydrogens and a p orbital of the carbon atom, which would lead to three MO's roughly at right angles to one another; but the remaining hydrogen would make only a poor overlap with the s orbital of the carbon, leading to a weak fourth bond. We know that the four C—H bonds in methane are in fact all equivalent, strong, and directed toward the corners of a regular tetrahedron (page 71).

To overcome this difficulty, a new principle was introduced, and it proved useful in many other cases too. It involves mixing a number of different AO's to yield an equal number of identical *hybrid* AO's. The process, known as the *hybridization of atomic orbitals*, has detailed mathematical justification. For methane— and indeed for the carbon atoms in aliphatic compounds generally—we need to mix one $2s$ and three $2p$ orbitals. The procedure is known as sp^3 *hybridization*. Its effect is to yield four equivalent orbitals directed tetrahedrally.

Each hybrid orbital has a large lobe in one direction and a much smaller one in the opposite direction, and it is only with the larger lobe that appreciable overlap with the $1s$ orbital of the hydrogen atom can occur. One such sp^3-hybridized AO only is fully represented in Fig. 3.4, the directions of the other three, which are identical in shape, being merely indicated. The carbon atom, after being first "prepared" in this way, can develop four MO's with the AO's of the four hydrogen atoms, and thus it can form four strong C—H bonds directed tetrahedrally. In all cases when a carbon atom is linked to four other atoms, we may suppose it to start from this sp^3-hybridized state.

When there are double bonds, a different type of hybridization must be invoked before the MO method can be applied. We suppose one s orbital of the carbon atom to be mixed with only two of its p orbitals, leaving the third p orbital unchanged. This sp^2 *hybridization* leads to three equivalent AO's making angles of $120°$ with each other; they all lie in the same plane, and the third p orbital is directed perpendicularly to this plane.

The situation is sketched in Fig. 3.5a. The simplest molecule which can be interpreted on this basis is that of ethylene, C_2H_4. We assume two carbon atoms to be in the sp^2-hybridized state, with three of the valence electrons in the three hybridized AO's and the fourth in the unchanged p orbital. These atoms and four hydrogens come together, and the AO's overlap to give five MO's forming five bonds in an arrangement suggested, in perspective,

figure 3.4

An sp³-hybridized atomic orbital. Only one of the four orbitals is shown in full; the tetrahedral directions of the others are indicated by arrows.

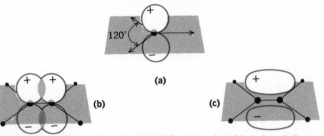

The directions of the trigonal sp^2-hybridized atomic orbitals in relation to the direction of the unused p orbital and the overlap of two p orbitals to yield a π type molecular orbital in ethylene.

by Fig. 3.5b. Ten electrons are accommodated in this way—three from each carbon and one from each hydrogen atom. Two electrons and two $2p$ orbitals remain on the two carbon atoms. Provided the latter are parallel, the AO's can overlap laterally as is suggested in Fig. 3.5b; and provided that they are also in phase, as is indicated by the $+$ and $-$ signs, they form a new kind of MO.

As represented in Fig. 3.5c, this MO has sausage-shaped regions of electron density above and below the C—C bond and with a nodal surface in the plane of the six atomic nuclei. In this orbital the remaining two electrons are paired, with a diminution of energy and therefore with an enhancement of the bonding force between the carbon atoms.

According to this interpretation, the ethylenic double bond, $>C{=}C<$, is not just two single bonds as the conventional bond diagram seems to imply. Rather, it consists of a true single bond, which uses an MO formed by the overlap of an sp^2-hybridized AO from each carbon atom, plus the new type of bond, which uses the MO formed by the overlap of the two p orbitals. The first, which may be regarded as an ordinary covalence, is known as a σ bond (Greek sigma); the second is known as a π bond.

These different names emphasize a significant difference of properties. If, in Fig. 3.5b, we were to rotate one half of the molecule about the C—C line, the σ bonding would not be affected. The π bonding, on the other hand, would be seriously impaired, because the p orbitals overlap effectively only when the two halves of the molecule are in the relative orientation shown. This explains the observation that a double bond between carbon atoms requires the four attached atoms to be coplanar, or nearly so, as are the hydrogen atoms in ethylene. There is no "free rotation" about a double bond. We now realize that rotation about a single bond is not quite free, but it does occur far more readily (see page 65).

Molecular-orbital theory uses the concept of sp^2-hybridized carbon to account for the bonding in benzene and other aromatic molecules. Figure 3.6a shows the scheme for the benzene molecule, which is seen in nearly edge-on perspective. Six carbon atoms, each sp^2-hybridized, arrange themselves in a regular hexagon, thus making full use of the $120°$ angles between their AO's. With the addition of six hydrogen atoms, this hexagon gives the benzene skeleton united by twelve σ bonds, six C—H and six C—C, around the ring. There remain six electrons and six unused p orbitals on the six carbon atoms. Lateral overlap will give rise to six MO's. Three of these are antibonding and do not interest us. In the other three MO's the six electrons are accommodated, with a lowering of energy, so that the MO's are bonding.

In Fig. 3.6b we have sketched only one of these bonding orbitals, the simplest of them. It has a nodal plane, in which $\psi = 0$, in the plane of the six carbon atoms, and it has two doughnut-shaped regions of electron density above and below the plane. It is important to notice that the six electrons in these three π orbitals are not localized between any particular pair of atoms. Instead, they range over the whole ring. To this aromatic sextet, as it is sometimes called, many of the peculiar properties of benzenoid compounds can be attributed.

The formation of true double bonds of the kind just described is largely confined to the elements of the first short period, and hence to the atoms C, N, and O. We shall come across a few exceptions to this rule later on, but we can perhaps exempt them by claiming that they are double bonds of a different kind. They involve π bonding, but not simply between two atoms each of which contributes a p orbital.

Various other forms of hybridization can occur, and the concept has value over a wide range of chemistry. We need mention only one other example. When one s and one p orbital are mixed, we get two sp-hybridized AO's which are directed at $180°$ to one another. This type of hybridization is used in an explanation of

figure 3.6

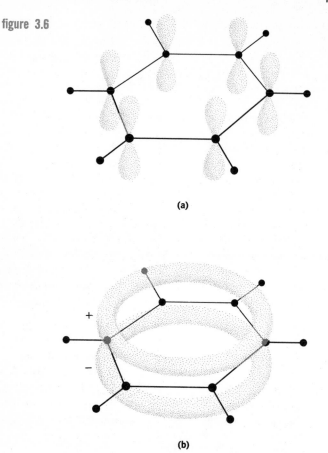

(a)

(b)

The molecular-orbital theory of the benzene molecule. For clarity in (a) the unused p orbitals on the carbon atoms are betokened by unrealistically narrow lobes; lateral overlap between these atomic orbitals leads to three bonding molecular orbitals of π type, the simplest of which is indicated in (b).

the triple bond in such molecules as acetylene, $HC\equiv CH$. Overlap of the sp orbitals gives a single σ bond between the carbon atoms. After also combining with the hydrogen atoms, each carbon still has two electrons and two unhybridized p orbitals at right angles to one another and to the direction of the C—C bond. Lateral overlap between the p orbitals leads to a pair of bonding MO's, in which the four electrons are absorbed. The triple bond therefore can be regarded as a σ bond plus two π bonds.

When we have difficulty in describing an unfamiliar object, it is a common trick to say that it is a cross between two things that are more familiar. To cite a famous example, a mule can be described as a cross between a horse and a donkey. This happens to be an exact description. So perhaps a better example for our present purpose—because of its inevitable inaccuracy—is to describe the game of hockey as a cross between golf and soccer. This tactic is used in the wave-mechanical treatment of molecules, and it can be very useful. One form of it appears in the valence-bond, or VB, approximation. This, like the MO approximation, can be applied in quantitative calculations, but again we shall concern ourselves with it only as a descriptive device.

The principle can be roughly outlined as follows: When two or more reasonable electronic formulas can be written for a molecule, the actual molecule is better described as a blend of—or a cross between—these formulas than by one of them alone. We shall not fully define what we mean by "reasonable"; but all the formulas must have the correct number of electrons, they must all have the atoms in nearly the same positions, and they must all have about the same energy. The examples we are about to give will help the reader to develop a feeling of what can get by.

Earlier in this chapter we wrote (5) as the electronic formula for the carbon dioxide molecule. It embodies the correct number, 16, of valence electrons, and each atom has a completed octet. We can write another formula (4) which also satisfies these conditions. [Closer inspection will show that the oxygen atoms in (4) carry formal charges, $\overset{+}{O}\equiv C-\overset{-}{O}$, but we do not need to draw attention to this here.] Symmetry allows us to write formula (6) as well—the "opposite" of (4).

$$|O\equiv C-\underset{\cdot\cdot}{O}| \qquad \langle\underset{\cdot\cdot}{O}=C=\underset{\cdot\cdot}{O}\rangle \qquad |\underset{\cdot\cdot}{O}-C\equiv O|$$

$$(4) \qquad\qquad (5) \qquad\qquad (6)$$

Though these formulas would require *slight* differences in the C—O distances (see Chap. 4), they would all have the three atoms collinear. So we have here three reasonable electronic formulas. The VB method assumes that the actual carbon dioxide molecule is represented by a blend, or mixture, of these three better than by any one of them singly. The molecule is said to undergo *resonance* between (4), (5), and (6), and it is more stable in consequence. We shall give some evidence for this enhanced stability in Chap. 4.

Another instructive example concerns the ionization of a carboxylic acid like acetic acid (7). Acetic acid, though weak compared with hydrochloric acid and the other strong "mineral acids," is relatively strong for an organic acid. Alcohol, for instance, is virtually devoid of acidic properties. While the acid itself is

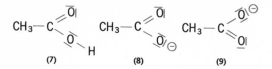

(7)   (8)   (9)

represented only by the one formula (7), two equivalent electronic formulas are valid for the acetate ion [(8) and (9)] produced when the acid ionizes. Resonance therefore occurs: the acetate ion is better considered as a blend of (8) and (9) than as either separately, and it thereby acquires extra stability. Hence the ionization is encouraged. The hypothetical anion which would result if a molecule of ethyl alcohol were to ionize would not be stabilized in this way, so that its ionization is not encouraged by resonance. Carboxylic acids are much more acidic than alcohols or phenols.

As a third example, we take the VB concept of the benzene molecule, C_6H_6. One of the early triumphs of organic chemistry was the discovery that the six carbon atoms are linked together into a ring, or more accurately, into a regular hexagon (10). In this formula only three bonds are shown at each carbon atom. The requisite four can be made up by making three of the six bonds double, as shown in conventionally simplified form in (11). But this formula is still not acceptable, because it embodies two different sorts of C—C bonds whereas all the chemical properties of benzene suggest that all six bonds round the ring are equivalent. Friedrich August Kekulé von Stradonitz (1829–1896), a German chemist, overcame this difficulty by adding formula (12) with the alternative arrangement of double and single bonds. He supposed that the bonds were in some sense oscillating between the two arrangements. The resonance (VB) concept uses the same idea in a different way: the bonds are not oscillating; the molecule is not sometimes like (11) and at other times like (12). Rather,

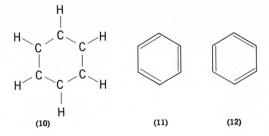

(10)   (11)   (12)

it is always the same, in an unchanging condition that is a blend of (11) and (12). The actual electronic formula is approximated better by taking it to be a hybrid of the two shown.

This reminds us of an essential point about resonance, a point we may emphasize by reverting to the classical analogy cited at the beginning of this section. A mule is not sometimes a horse, sometimes a donkey. It is, all the time, a new sort of beast that can be approximately considered to be an "average" of horse and donkey: it is a hybrid.

We shall revert to the resonance concept in the next chapter, where a more detailed consideration of molecular structure will enable us to gain a fuller understanding of its value.

valence among second-row elements

For the elements of the first row* of the periodic table (lithium to fluorine) the valence electrons are those of the second shell; as the $2s$ and then the three $2p$ orbitals are filled, the octet is completed. The chemical behavior of these elements, and particularly of carbon, nitrogen, and oxygen, is based on this octet. One consequence is that these elements can never have a true valence higher than 4. Four electron pairs make up the octet, and more electrons cannot be accommodated in the second shell. Nitrogen in ammonium salts (such as NH_4Cl) appears at first sight to be quinquevalent, as was formerly supposed; but, as we saw on page 40, the covalence is 4 and there is a positive charge on the NH_4^+ ion, which then engages in an electrovalent attachment to a chlorine ion.

In elements of the second row, sodium to chlorine and beyond, genuinely higher valences can arise. This is easily comprehensible

---

* Some authors regard H and He as constituting the first row (or period) of the table; then Li to Ne would be in the second row and Na to Ar in the third. However, the periodicity is so rudimentary in H and He that it is permissible to adopt the scheme used here.

because we are now dealing with the third shell, where there are nine orbitals—one $3s$, three $3p$, and five $3d$. We are not restricted to the octet. Two simple examples will serve:

1. Phosphorus pentachloride, PCl_5. Five chlorine atoms are covalently linked to the phosphorus, and the grouping round this last atom comprises 10 electrons. Hybridization of one $3s$, three $3p$, and one of the $3d$ orbitals can yield five appropriate AO's.

2. Sulfur hexafluoride, SF_6. Six fluorine atoms are covalently bonded to the sulfur; the group of 12 valence electrons are accommodated in 6 d^2sp^3-hybridized MO's formed from AO's of the sulfur atom.

Derivatives of phosphoric acid, H_3PO_4, have biological importance, and their electronic formulation is of interest. For the acid itself, the simplest bond diagram is (13), the bond to the nonhydroxylic oxygen atom being formally dative. This formula gives the phosphorus and each of the oxygen atoms a completed octet of electrons. It may not be wholly adequate, because there is evidence for some double-bond character in the P—O bonds.

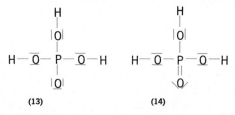

(13)   (14)

This could arise if use were made of one or more of the d orbitals of the phosphorus atom to form MO's which could accommodate lone-pair electrons from the oxygen atoms. One possible formula embodying this effect is (14). In VB terms there might be resonance between (13) and such forms as (14). As between different phosphate derivatives, the amount of resonance stabilization arising in this way may vary, and consequently the strength of the P—O bonds may vary in different compounds (see page 129).

We have hinted at exceptions to the useful rule that double bonds can be formed only by elements of the first short period. The participation of forms such as (14) is a probable example. George Wald has suggested that this exceptional behavior may occur because the phosphorus atom is just small enough to hold the extra π electrons. We must, however, emphasize that the double bonding here differs appreciably from that occurring in simple ethylenic compounds as we described it on page 47, where the π orbital is formed by overlap of two p orbitals of neighboring carbon atoms. Any such bonding in the P—O system depends on MO's formed by the overlap of a p orbital of the oxygen atom with d orbitals of the phosphorus. The situation is considerably more complicated, and the bonding is probably less strong.

Similar problems arise in the molecules of sulfuric acid and the sulfates.

4

the quantitative study
of molecular structure

We explained in Chap. 1 how a sophisticated study of chemical properties led to a remarkably detailed knowledge of molecular structures. As was also emphasized, this knowledge was incomplete. Though the water molecule was confidently believed to consist of two hydrogens linked to an oxygen atom (H—O—H), its actual dimensions—the distances between the hydrogens and the oxygen, for instance, and the angle subtended by them—were unknown. Nor was anything known about the strength of the bonds.

In some cases, to be sure, something was known about the *general* shape of the molecule. There was good reason for believing that four atoms attached to a carbon atom lay in the directions of the corners of a tetrahedron (page 8). Whether the tetrahedron was regular or not could only be guessed: when the four atoms were all the same, as in CH_4 or CCl_4, the tetrahedron was expected to be regular. In that case the H—C—H or Cl—C—Cl bond angles would have the value required by the trigonometric consideration that their cosines must all be $-\frac{1}{3}$, that is, slightly less than 110°. If, on the other hand, the four atoms differed, as in CH_3Cl, the angles might well differ; but whether this was really so and, if so, by how much were quite unknown.

During the period 1920 to 1935 a number of physical methods for gaining direct answers to some of the questions implied above were discovered. These methods have been applied assiduously, so that a great mass of information on *molecular properties* is now available. The information is continually being augmented and made more exact as the methods are developed. Our knowledge of molecules has been revolutionized. It has advanced from the qualitative and descriptive to the quantitative and metrical. This has encouraged work on the theory of molecules, which we outlined in Chap. 3.

At least half a dozen physical methods are now employed for studying various aspects of molecular structure. Three of them are outstandingly useful: (1) molecular spectra, (2) electron diffraction by gases and vapors, and (3) x-ray diffraction by crystals. We shall describe these three methods briefly, give some idea of their scope and limitations, and illustrate the results they yield.

1. The *spectra of molecules* are much more complicated than those of atoms (see Chap. 2), and their complexity increases rapidly with the size of the molecule. Anything like a full elucidation of the spectrum is possible only with very simple molecules comprising a few atoms. Diatomic molecules are the easiest to study. When there are more than two atoms, difficulties increase rapidly, although molecules with several atoms can be usefully studied in favorable circumstances.

Besides the energy connected with the state of its electrons, a molecule possesses energy by virtue of its rotation about its center of mass and by virtue of the vibration of its atoms relative to one another. These aspects of the molecule are the principal features of interest to the chemist who wishes to study molecular structure.

When we have to deal dynamically with the rotation of a body, an important characteristic is the *moment of inertia* with respect to the axis of rotation. In general, an object could rotate about any one of an infinite number of possible axes; but mathematically, for a linear molecule, these reduce to two principal axes which are equivalent and perpendicular to each other and to the length of the molecule. For a nonlinear molecule, they reduce to three principal axes. Accordingly, the molecule has one principal moment of inertia only if it is linear; otherwise, it has three. HCl is an example of a linear molecule whose rotation is characterized by a single moment of inertia; H_2O and CH_4 are examples of nonlinear molecules with three principal moments of inertia.

A successful study of the spectrum due to a molecule will tell us the value (or values) of its moment (or moments) of inertia. In suitably simple cases this information enables us to calculate the molecular dimensions. For example, the moment of inertia of the HCl molecule is 2.72×10^{-40} cgs unit. (There are two isotopes of chlorine, and this value applies to the species of HCl involving the Cl^{35} isotope.) By a well-known formula of dynamics, the moment of inertia of a body consisting of two masses M_H and M_{Cl}, a distance d apart, is equal to

$$\frac{d^2(M_H \times M_{Cl})}{M_H + M_{Cl}}$$

The masses of the atoms are obtained by dividing the respective atomic weights by the Avogadro number (p. 15), so that we have

1   $$2.72 \times 10^{-40} = \frac{d^2(1 \times 35)}{36 \times 6 \times 10^{23}}$$

whence

2   $$d = 1.3 \times 10^{-8} \text{ cm} = 1.3 \text{ Å}$$

The situation is more complicated with a triatomic molecule, but from the three principal moments of inertia of the water molecule [about 1.00, 1.91, and 2.98 (each) $\times 10^{-40}$ cgs unit] the bond lengths and angles can be derived. (Two sets of dimensions are mathematically possible, but only one of them is chemically acceptable and compatible with all our other information.) Since spectroscopic measurements can be made with high accuracy, the molecular dimensions derived in this way are generally of high precision. Three or four places of decimals (Å) for bond lengths can often be justified. On the other hand, as we have already stressed, the method is applicable only to small molecules. It could never be applied to a molecule even of the complexity of that of glucose, $C_6H_{12}O_6$.

Molecules can also vibrate. For a diatomic molecule the vibration reduces to a simple to-and-fro motion of the atoms along the line joining them. The system closely resembles that of two ordinary weights linked by a coil spring. Spectroscopic study enables us to determine the frequency of the actual molecular vibration, and this in turn leads to a knowledge of the strength of the bonds between the atoms, as we shall explain in more detail later.

2. *Electron diffraction* depends on the principle (page 22) that a moving particle is associated with a wavelength $\lambda = h/mv$. For this method we need a beam of electrons moving in a vacuum, all with the same velocity v and therefore with the same wavelength.

This beam is allowed to pass through a fine jet of the vapor of the substance we wish to study, and then to fall onto a photographic plate or film. (Precautions must be taken to ensure that the jet of vapor does not spoil the vacuum.)

Some of the electrons in the beam are scattered by the molecules of the jet; and because of the wave nature of the electrons, the developed plate shows a pattern of concentric rings around the central spot due to the undeflected electron beam. This is the *diffraction pattern*. By careful study of this pattern, and with a knowledge of the wavelength of the electrons used, information on the size and shape of the molecules can be derived. Recent refinements have rendered this method almost as accurate as molecular spectroscopy, but again its useful application is restricted to simple molecules that can be obtained in the gaseous condition.

As an example we may cite carbon tetrachloride, CCl_4, which has been frequently studied as a test of the method's capabilities. The diffraction pattern can be interpreted as due to a molecule with four chlorine atoms arranged in a regularly tetrahedral fashion around a carbon atom, and a fairly recent analysis yields a value of 1.766 ± 0.003 Å for the C—Cl distance.

3. *X-ray diffraction* can also be used with gases, though it is less convenient than electron diffraction. However, x-rays prove to be especially well adapted for the study of molecules in crystals, and some thousands of substances have now been studied in this way.

In the most powerful version of this method, a small single crystal of the substance is placed in a narrow beam of x-rays. These x-rays must be monochromatic, i.e., they must all have the same wavelength. The crystal then acts as a three-dimensional diffraction grating for the x-rays, so that a photographic film placed to receive the scattered beam shows a pattern of sharp spots, on development.

A complete study of the x-ray diffraction pattern calls for a series of exposures over a range of different orientations of the crystal. Quantitative information about the pattern takes the form of measurements of the intensities of a large number of different diffraction spots. The task of determining the structure of the molecules of which the crystal is composed varies, for technical reasons, from the easy to the impossible in different cases.

In favorable cases molecules with as many as 40 to 50 atoms have often been elucidated. After massive effort, a few much larger ones have been successfully analyzed, vitamin B_{12}, $C_{63}H_{88}O_{14}N_{14}PCo$, being the most celebrated example. At the time of writing (1964), the molecule of one protein, myoglobin, has been largely solved by persistent and protracted x-ray work.

When an x-ray analysis has been successfully completed, the relative positions of all the atoms in the molecule are known. Hence we can easily calculate the bond lengths and all other interatomic distances and the bond angles. We also know the complete stereochemistry of the molecule. Usually the positions of the hydrogen atoms are excepted, since they have only a small effect on the total x-ray scattering, but even they can sometimes be located with less precision. The accuracy attainable in x-ray analysis depends on the complexity of the molecule. In very favorable cases, interatomic distances can be determined to within ± 0.005 Å, but the accuracy is often less than this, perhaps only ± 0.05 Å.

There are some other physical methods that can be applied and some other molecular properties that can be useful in furthering our understanding of molecular structure. We shall mention some of these later as the occasion requires. Generally, these additional methods and properties are less important than the ones just described.

the potential-energy diagram for a diatomic molecule

Before we consider the results given by these physical methods, we may ask what a molecule is like when studied from this point of view. A valuable insight into the behavior of a diatomic molecule like H_2 or HCl or NO may be derived from its *potential-energy diagram*. This is a graph in which the energy E of a molecule is plotted against the distance d between the two atomic nuclei, and it has the general shape shown in Fig. 4.1. Since the two atoms are to form a covalent bond, an attractive force operates between them, so that the energy diminishes, the closer they come together. This is signified by the right-hand part of the graph, which falls as d decreases.

This fall cannot continue indefinitely; for if it did, the two nuclei would come into coincidence with $d = 0$. This does not happen because a counteracting repulsive force begins to operate when

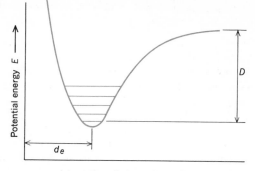

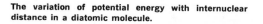

The variation of potential energy with internuclear distance in a diatomic molecule.

the atoms get close enough together. We can understand this by realizing that the covalent force of attraction (which was discussed in Chap. 3) will be opposed by the repulsion between the two positively charged nuclei, as well as by the repulsion between the other electrons of each atom. Thus the energy curve has the shape shown, with a minimum corresponding to the distance between the atoms at which attraction and repulsion just balance one another.

By an analogy, which is in this respect fairly apt, we might consider a pair of weights lying on a smooth table and connected by a coil spring. Since the spring resists both stretching and compression, the system will be in static equilibrium when the weights are a certain distance apart. Work would have to be done either to compress the spring, so as to force the weights closer together, or to stretch it, so as to pull them farther apart. Either way, the potential energy would be increased; the equilibrium position is one of minimum energy. This is also true for the diatomic molecule, and the equilibrium distance d_e, shown in Fig. 4.1, is therefore an important characteristic of the molecule which we may hope to measure experimentally.

When a diatomic molecule vibrates, the distance between its atoms oscillates to and fro about the equilibrium value d_e. The point on the diagram, which represents the condition of the molecule at any instant, slides backward and forward along the curve on either side of the minimum. When the vibrations are of small amplitude, the motion will be simple harmonic and the curve parabolic. In dynamical terms the restoring force is proportional to the displacement, or in mathematical form,

Restoring force $= f \times (d - d_e)$

Known as the *force constant*, f is an important characteristic of the vibration, since it measures the force for a given strain of the bond. It can be determined from the molecular spectrum, and its value, which varies for different molecules, is of the order of 10^6 dynes/cm. (Needless to say, if the bond were literally stretched by 1 cm, the molecule would long since have ceased to exist. The figure given is like quoting the price of gold as so many billion dollars per megaton.) Force constants are one useful measure of the strength of a bond.

There is one important difference between the vibrations of a molecule and those of a system of weights and springs. Ordinary dynamics fails for very small bodies, and for atoms and molecules it must be replaced by wave mechanics. A consequence of this is that the vibrational energy of a molecule is *quantized*, as is the electronic energy of an atom or, indeed, the rotational energy of a molecule. The vibrational energy cannot, therefore, have just any value; it must be in one or another of a series of discrete levels.

It turns out that the permissible values for the vibrational energy E_{vib} of a diatomic molecule are those given by the formula

$E_{vib} = h\omega(v + \frac{1}{2})$

where h is Planck's constant (page 22), ω is the frequency of the molecular vibration, and v (in this context) is the vibrational quantum number, which may have whole-number values 0, 1, 2, etc. A curious feature of this equation is the appearance of $v + \frac{1}{2}$ where one might have expected only v. This is a result of wave mechanics, and, like the quantization, it has no analogy in the mechanics of ordinary-sized bodies. It has an important consequence: even in the lowest possible state of vibration, where $v = 0$, there is still some vibrational energy, $\frac{1}{2}h\omega$.

In other words, a molecule can never be at rest with respect to its vibrations; at the absolute zero of temperature, when as much energy as possible has been drained away, this residue remains. It is known as *zero-point energy*. We have plenty of evidence for the genuineness of the effect. In a theoretical perspective, it can be seen as a consequence of the uncertainty principle (page 21). If there were no zero-point energy, the positions and momenta of the atoms in a molecule could be exactly defined. With zero-point energy persisting, the uncertainty is preserved.

The vibration frequency is connected with the force constant by the simple formula of dynamics

$$\omega = \tfrac{1}{2}\pi \sqrt{\frac{f(M_1 + M_2)}{M_1 M_2}}$$

where M_1 and M_2 are the masses of the atoms. From the spectrum of the substance in the gaseous state, ω can be determined; hence, the masses of the atoms being known, the force constant f can be calculated. For hydrogen chloride ω is about 8.3×10^{13} sec^{-1}, whence f is found to be about 4.5×10^5 dynes/cm, as the reader should easily be able to confirm.

These considerations suggest a possible addition to our potential-energy diagram, Fig. 4.1. The vibrational levels can be indicated by drawing horizontal lines across the curve. The lowest such line corresponds to the zero-point vibration; the interatomic distance oscillates between values marked by the ends of the line. In a typical case the extent of the vibration is about 0.1 Å on either side of d_e. Similarly, vibrations of wider amplitude in the higher levels are indicated by the higher lines. We notice that the molecule is never actually in the situation corresponding to the minimum of the curve; for if it were, there would be no vibration. In fact, the interatomic distance we derive from the moment of inertia is an average of the constantly changing value of d as the molecule vibrates. So long as the vibrations are of small amplitude, however, the difference between d_e and the average d derived experimentally is not serious.

As we stated earlier, the lower part of the potential-energy curve is parabolic. Deviations from this symmetrical shape must occur at higher vibrational levels. There is no limit to the amount by which the bond can be extended, because the attractive force rapidly grows weaker; but as the atoms are pressed together, more and more severe repulsion occurs. Therefore, the curve takes on the form shown in the upper parts of Fig. 4.1. To the right it tends to level off and become horizontal as the molecule dissociates into separate atoms which no longer attract one another.

The vertical height between the lowest vibrational level and the level at which the curve becomes horizontal is marked on the diagram as D. This represents the work necessary to dissociate the molecule. This *dissociation energy* D is an alternative measure of the strength of the bond. It also can sometimes be determined from the molecular spectrum.

To recapitulate, the structure of a diatomic molecule is defined by a single quantity or, to use a more technical term, *parameter*. This is d_e, the interatomic distance in the hypothetical state of zero vibration, or, if we take note of the necessity for zero-point vibration, some sort of average value of d which will differ but little from d_e. If we care to widen the meaning of the word "structure," we can define two other properties: the force constant f and the dissociation energy D. Both these have close connections with the strength of the bond. All three parameters can be determined experimentally from the spectrum.

polyatomic molecules Molecules having more than two atoms are structurally more complicated, and we need not consider them in as much detail. A few examples will show some of the special features of polyatomic molecules. Water has a triatomic molecule, with its three atoms not all in a straight line. Here we need three parameters to define the structure. For these we could choose the distances between each of the three pairs of atoms; the atomic centers constitute a triangle, and a triangle can be described by the lengths of its sides.

There is, however, an alternative description—by two sides and the included angle; and this seems more natural to a chemist, because he thinks of this molecule as having two hydrogen atoms bonded to the one oxygen (but not to one another), with a certain angle between the bonds at the oxygen atom. The distance between the two hydrogen atoms would normally be regarded as a consequence of the bond angle at the oxygen, rather than of any direct interaction between them. For this chemical reason, and not by any geometric logic, a molecule such as H_2O is always described structurally by two bond lengths and one bond angle.

The values are in fact 0.96 Å for each O—H bond and 105° for the H—O—H angle. In this case the triangle is isosceles.

This sort of description is applied generally to all molecules whose structures we wish to record. We state the distances between neighboring atoms that we suppose to be bonded to each other (bond lengths); and when two atoms are each bonded to a third, we state the bond angle.

There is a subtler kind of parameter which we sometimes need to describe a molecule in which there is a chain of more than three atoms. Figure 4.2 represents a molecule consisting of four atoms A, B, D, and E. Following the preceding paragraph, we can declare three bond lengths (A—B, B—D, and D—E) and two bond angles (A—B—D and B—D—E), but the precise shape of the molecule will still not be defined. By twisting the D—E bond through 180° about the B—D line, the zigzag shape of Fig. 4.2a could be changed into the crescent shape of Fig. 4.2b. Theoretically, there could be an infinite number of other *conformations*, as they are termed, between (a) and (b) as the angle of twist is gradually altered. In fact, however, the number of possibilities is limited, though sometimes they are of practical interest.

When the atoms B and D are carbons, and when the bond between them is single, twisting about this bond occurs fairly readily, so that different conformations are easily interconverted. Except in special circumstances, we do not, then, need to consider the possibility of different isomeric forms. One conformation will stand for all other possibilities.

To twist a molecule about a double C—C bond is much more difficult, however. Two arrangements of the chain, corresponding either to Fig. 4.2a (0° twist) or to Fig. 4.2b (180°

figure 4.2

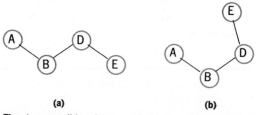

(a)   (b)

The two possible planar conformations of a chain of four atoms.

twist), are stable, but a strong resistance has to be overcome before one form can be twisted into the other. This was proved by classical organic chemistry, which recognized as different and distinct substances compounds with formulas such as (1) and (2).

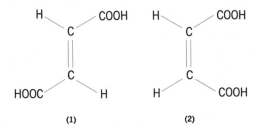

(1)   (2)

Fumaric acid has the structure represented by formula (1) and is known as the *trans isomer*, because it has the significant groups on opposite sides, while maleic acid (2) is known as the *cis isomer*, with the groups on the same side of the molecule. The molecular-orbital interpretation (page 48) explains the absence of free rotation about the double bond.

The possible vibrations of a polyatomic molecule are more varied than the simple stretching of the bond in a diatomic molecule, as we considered it in the preceding section. It is still possible for each bond to undergo *stretching vibrations*. These can lead to various combinations, as, for instance, when the extension of one bond is in phase, or out of phase, with the extension of the next bond. In addition, there may be vibrations of a different sort when bond angles change though bond lengths remain constant. These are known as *bending vibrations*. They, too, can be studied spectroscopically. Generally they occur rather more easily than bond stretchings and have lower frequencies. For instance, the vibration of the water molecule that involves changes of the H—O—H angle on either side of 105° has a frequency of about 4×10^{13} sec^{-1}, compared with about 10^{14} for the O—H stretching, and the force constant is about ten times smaller. Still weaker types of vibration involve twisting of the parts of a molecule about a bond while the angles and lengths remain constant.

We can now state a useful rule that there are three ways of distorting a molecule, by (1) stretching, (2) bending, and (3) twisting its bonds, and that the resistance to distortion by these means runs in the sequence 1 > 2 > 3.

the dipole
moment

Every molecule contains positive and negative electrical charges—atomic nuclei and electrons. Though in a neutral molecule the numbers of these opposite charges must exactly balance each other, their effective "centers of gravity" need not coincide. When they do not, there results some separation of electric charge; one end of the molecule will have a net positive charge, the other a net negative charge. When this happens, the molecule is said to be *polar*. It has an (electric) *dipole moment*. When placed in an electrostatic field, the molecule will tend to turn itself into the direction of the field, just as a compass needle, owing to its magnetic moment, will turn itself into the direction of the earth's magnetic field.

By various physical methods, preferably applied to the substance in the gaseous form, the dipole moment of the molecules of a substance can be deduced. In principle, a polar molecule is equivalent to equal positive and negative charges of magnitude e separated by a distance d. The dipole moment μ is then defined by the equation

$$\mu = e \times d$$

With e in the electrostatic units of charge and d in centimeters, μ is generally of the order of 10^{-18} cm-esu. For the water molecule it is 1.82×10^{-18} unit. Such quantities are conveniently expressed in terms of the *Debye unit* D, which is 10^{-18} cm-esu, so that for water $\mu = 1.82$ D.

Before giving some other examples, we may consider what kinds of molecules might be expected to possess zero or nonzero moments. Any simple molecule of high symmetry will have a zero dipole moment.* Examples are the diatomic molecules with identical atoms, such as H_2, O_2, and Cl_2, and certain polyatomic molecules whose structures are well balanced, such as CH_4, CCl_4 and benzene, C_6H_6. On the other hand, any molecule which is recognizably "one-sided" will have a nonzero moment. Examples are HCl, H_2O, CH_3Cl (methyl chloride), CH_3COOH (acetic acid), and C_6H_5Cl (chlorobenzene).

---

* The strict definition of symmetry is a technical matter that need not concern us here. Certain molecules may have quite high symmetry and still be dipolar. The water molecule, for example, has two planes of symmetry and a 2-fold axis. On the other hand, CH_4, though it lacks a center of symmetry, has high symmetry and is nonpolar.

We may consider the first example in more detail and in reference to its electronic formula, H—$\overline{\underline{Cl}}$|. A simple, if naive, way to do this is to think of the electron pair, which constitutes the bond, as being inequitably shared; it is rather more closely held by the chlorine atom than by the hydrogen. In this way the hydrogen atom acquires a *partial* positive charge, which may be signified by using the Greek letter delta ($\delta+$), and the chlorine acquires a partial negative charge ($\delta-$). This effect is general whenever a covalent bond is formed between two dissimilar atoms. The atoms differ in *electronegativity*, or the power of attracting the pair of bonding electrons. In our example chlorine is more electronegative than is hydrogen; the electrons are drawn some way from the hydrogen toward the chlorine, and the molecule has a dipole moment in the sense $\overset{\delta+}{H}$—$\overset{\delta-}{Cl}$.

When a dative covalence is formed, there is a more marked separation of charge between the two atoms concerned; formally, as we showed on page 38, full charges are produced. So we should expect molecules with a dative bond to have large dipole moments. This is generally true. For instance, the amine oxide, $(CH_3)_3\overset{\oplus}{N}$—$\overset{\ominus}{O}$, which we took as our example of dative covalence, has $\mu = 5.0$ D. Of course, if there are several such dative bonds in the same molecule, they may cancel one another's effects and produce a zero moment overall. We shall return to the subject of dipole moments in the next section.

the dimensions of some important molecules Since the 1930's, the application of the physical methods described in the preceding sections has yielded a great mass of information about the structures of molecules, and this information is being continually amended and supplemented. In due course it finds its way into tabulations, such as the "Special Publication No. 11" of the Chemical Society of London, where it is more conveniently accessible than in the original papers.*

A study of the accumulated data enables us to detect trends and guiding principles which are useful in systematizing the data as well as in allowing us to make reasonable estimates of the dimensions of molecules not yet actually measured. We shall discuss these generalizations later. First we describe the sizes and shapes

* A supplementary "No. 18" has recently been issued.

table 4.1 **some diatomic molecules**

MOLECULE	H_2	N_2	O_2	Cl_2	HCl	CO
d, Å	0.742	1.097	1.208	1.989	1.274	1.128

of a few simple molecules that are of basic importance, especially in biological systems.

We have explained that a diatomic molecule is dimensionally characterized by a single parameter, the bond length d. Some examples are given in Table 4.1.

A triatomic molecule is in general characterized by three parameters: two bond lengths and a bond angle. Molecules which have the bond angle 180° are linear, and they are usually classified together. Examples are CO_2 (carbon dioxide) and N_2O (nitrous oxide). CO_2 is symmetrical, with each C...O distance equal to 1.16 Å. (In a convenient abbreviation, this is often written C—O = 1.16 Å.) N_2O is unsymmetrical: the atoms lie in the sequence N—N—O, with N—N = 1.13 and N—O = 1.19 Å. Some examples of symmetrical, nonlinear triatomic molecules are given in Table 4.2, which also lists values for the dipole moments.

Ammonia has a tetratomic molecule NH_3, whose structure is important not only in its own right but also because many biologically essential molecules are *substitution products* of ammonia, that is to say, one or more of the hydrogen atoms of ammonia has been replaced by an organic group of some sort. The most obvious guess would be that the NH_3 molecule might have the shape of a flat, equilateral triangle with the nitrogen atom at the center and a hydrogen at each corner. The H—N—H angles would then all be 120°. In fact, the molecule is pyramidal, as we saw on page 46; the hydrogens do indeed lie at the corners of an equilateral triangle which constitutes the base of the pyramid, but the nitrogen lies about 0.4 Å above the center of the base. The parameters are N—H = 1.01 Å and H—N—H = 107°.

As shown in Table 4.2, all the nonlinear, triatomic molecules have nonzero dipole moments. We shall consider the water molecule in more detail from this point of view. Oxygen is more electronegative than hydrogen, with the result that each O—H bond has a partial separation of charges according to the simple concept outlined on page 69. The sense of this separation is shown

table 4.2 **nonlinear triatomic molecules**

MOLECULE	d (BOTH BONDS), Å	BOND ANGLE, DEGREES	DIPOLE MOMENT, D
H_2O	0.96	105	1.82
H_2S	1.33	93	1.0
O_3 (ozone)	1.28	117	0.5
NO_2 (nitrogen dioxide)	1.19	134	0.4

in Fig. 4.3a. If the two O—H bonds were collinear, their individual moments would cancel one another. Since they make an angle of 105°, there is a net dipole moment in the direction of the arrow. This can be derived by applying the principle of the parallelogram of forces to the two bond moments as suggested in Fig. 4.3b. In more technical language the overall dipole moment, which is what we observe, can be regarded as the *vector sum* of the two bond moments. This principle can be applied to more complicated molecules.

Next we turn to some simple organic molecules starting with methane, CH_4. Long ago the organic chemists deduced that the methane structure must be tetrahedral (page 8). Physical methods have confirmed that deduction. They have also proved that the tetrahedron is strictly regular, with all the H—C—H angles equal to $109\frac{1}{2}°$, which was originally no more than a reasonable guess. All the C—H distances are 1.09 Å.

A peculiarity of carbon compounds—and one which renders carbon chemistry unique—is the facility with which carbon atoms may be linked together into chains (see page 124). The first such *homologue* of methane, CH_4, is ethane, C_2H_6, or $CH_3 \cdot CH_3$. This molecule can be looked on as methane in which one of the hydrogen atoms has been replaced by the methyl group, CH_3, and its

figure 4.3

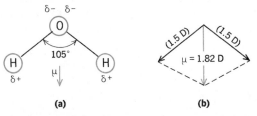

(a) (b)

Partial charges, bond moments, and the overall dipole moment of a water molecule.

structure is very similar. The C—H distances and the H—C—H angles are almost exactly the same, while the C—C distance is 1.54 Å. With the ethane molecule, we need another parameter to complete our description; for there is the possibility (page 66) of twisting the one methyl group with respect to the other.

In other words, we need to consider the conformation. While twisting is quite easy, the molecule in fact adopts a preferred conformation which is that suggested by Fig. 4.4a. The sketch is further elucidated by the diagram of Fig. 4.4c, where we are look- ing along the C—C direction and see the hydrogen atoms of the nearer methyl group exactly between those of the farther-away one. This is often known as the *staggered conformation*. The other simple arrangement, shown in Fig. 4.4b and d, is known as the *eclipsed conformation*. It has the hydrogens of one methyl group directly opposite those of the other; it is less stable, and the ethane molecule avoids it.

These facts concerning the conformation of the ethane molecule are not, in themselves, very important for our present purposes; but they provide an example of a principle that applies in many biological molecules, and notably in those of the fats. The prin- ciple can be illustrated by the simplest molecule containing a chain of four single-bonded carbon atoms, that of normal butane (n-butane, $CH_3 \cdot CH_2 \cdot CH_2 \cdot CH_3$).

The problem of conformation, so far as the carbon atoms are concerned, is just that set out in Fig. 4.2 if the atoms A, B, D, and E are now supposed to be carbons. This molecule can adopt var- ious shapes by twisting about the central bond. Its most stable form is that shown in Fig. 4.2a, with the staggered arrangement at the bond and the chain taking on the form of a planar zigzag. (The chain is as extended as possible while maintaining the bond angles, and all atoms shown are in the plane of the paper.) This is generally true of long-chain molecules of this kind. We may take as an example the $C_{17}H_{35}$ chain which occurs in stearic acid and in many fats. By twisting (or internal rotation) about each single C—C bond, such a chain can adopt a great variety of shapes overall. (Since the molecule vibrates, it probably does so, especially if the environment allows scope for such "writhings.") Its *most stable* shape, however, is that with all-staggered confor- mations at every bond.

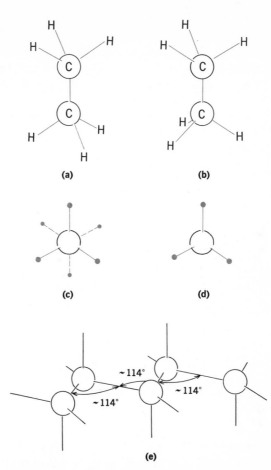

(a)   **(b)**

(c)   **(d)**

~114°   ~114°   ~114°

(e)

The ethane molecule in its (a) and (c) staggered and (b) and (d) eclipsed conformations. (e) The planar, zigzag conformation of a chain of singly bonded carbon atoms.

A section of the chain is sketched in Fig. 4.4e, where it will be seen that this arrangement brings the carbon atoms into a planar zigzag and puts the greatest possible distance between the ends of the chain. In the crystalline state, in which the packing of the molecules does not encourage over-much writhing, stearic acid has its chain in this extended form. The C—C—C angles are about 114°, rather greater than the tetrahedral value of 110°; and so, with C—C distances always about 1.54 Å, the distances between alternate carbon atoms are about 2.5 Å.

The molecule of ethylene, $CH_2{=}CH_2$, introduces a new feature: the double bond between carbon atoms (see page 47). This molecule has all its six atoms in one plane; the C—C distance is 1.34 Å, the C—H distances are all about 1.07 Å, and the H—C—H and C—C—H angles are all 120°. The double bond is considerably shorter than the single bond. The angles differ, too. Four single bonds around a carbon atom are directed toward the corners of a regular (or nearly regular) tetrahedron, giving bond angles of about 110°; but when the atom engages in one double bond, all the interbond angles are about 120°.

As we shall describe in Chap. 5, proteins have molecules built by the linking together of a large number of molecules of *amino acids*. For this reason great interest attaches to the structural details of the amino acids themselves, and especially to those of the simple *polypeptides* which result when a small number of amino acid units combine. We can illustrate some structural principles by reference to the simplest amino acid, glycine, and the simplest polypeptide, glycylglycine.

Formally, glycine is aminoacetic acid; for it has a molecule in which one of the hydrogen atoms of the methyl group in acetic acid has been replaced by the amino group, NH_2: NH_2CH_2COOH. This was the original, and obvious, formula for glycine. Later, plenty of evidence was discovered to prove that the formula is $\overset{+}{N}H_3CH_2CO\overset{-}{O}$; a proton has been transferred from the COOH group at one end of the molecule to the NH_2 group at the other end, producing a sort of "internal ionization." This type of structure, which is the normal condition of most amino acids, is known as a *zwitterion*.

Analysis of crystalline glycine by x-rays has confirmed this structure and given the molecular dimensions shown in Fig. 4.5a. The four atoms of carbon and oxygen are coplanar; but by a twist about the C—C bond, the nitrogen atom is put out of this plane by rather less than 0.5 Å. As would be expected from the VB considerations given on page 51, the two C—O distances are virtually identical. Though hydrogen atoms are harder to locate by x-ray diffraction, they have in this case been detected with sufficient certainty to show that three of them are linked to the nitrogen atom, as is required by the zwitterion.

figure 4.5

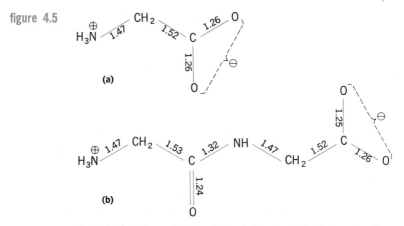

Dimensions of the molecules of (a) glycine, and (b) glycylglycine. Since the structural analysis of glycylglycine is a comparatively early one, and therefore of rather lower accuracy, the bond lengths in (b) have been slightly modified to bring them into conformity with the lengths of corresponding bonds in a number of other polypeptides which have been more recently measured with greater precision.

Amino acid molecules link themselves together to form a polypeptide by combination between the $\overset{+}{N}H_3$ group of one molecule and the $C\overset{-}{OO}$ group of the other, with loss of the elements of water. For example, the union of two molecules of glycine to yield glycylglycine follows the equation

$$\overset{+}{N}H_3CH_2CO\overset{-}{O} + \overset{+}{N}H_3CH_2CO\overset{-}{O} \rightarrow$$
$$\overset{+}{N}H_3CH_2CO—NHCH_2CO\overset{-}{O} + H_2O$$

The new bond between CO and NH is known as the *peptide linkage*. The molecule of a dipeptide like glycylglycine has the dimensions shown in Fig. 4.5b. The C—N distance of the peptide linkage is noticeably shorter than in the other C—N bond. The four atoms directly bonded to the carbon and nitrogen atoms of the peptide link are coplanar. Indeed, all the carbon, nitrogen, and oxygen atoms in the molecule are coplanar except for the $\overset{+}{N}H_3$ group, which again lies out of the general plane, as in glycine itself. The skeleton of the molecule consists of a planar zigzag chain like that in the long hydrocarbon chains mentioned above.

These structures have been determined for the solid state. We emphasize again that the overall shape of such a molecule can be changed rather easily by allowing small twists about each single bond, and this twisting may happen in solution. Nevertheless, the planar zigzag arrangement represents the most stable situation. This is relevant for an understanding of the polypeptide chains in protein molecules (page 112).

A feature of carbon chemistry is the ease with which chains of atoms can link up with themselves to form closed rings of atoms. This possibility gives rise to the complexities of alicyclic, aromatic, and heterocyclic compounds. In our survey of representative molecular structures we shall cite only a few examples of six-membered rings. Rings with different numbers of atoms also occur; five-membered rings are especially common. Six atoms, however, represent the commonest and most stable ring.

With carbon atoms each bonded to four others (i.e., with the atoms in the sp^3-hybridized state and the bonds directed tetrahedrally) the simplest ring molecule is that of cyclohexane, C_6H_{12}, whose structure is shown in Fig. 4.6a. This (alicyclic) molecule, which consists of a chain of six CH_2 groups linked into a ring, has the specially favorable feature that each C—C single bond is able to maintain its staggered conformation (page 72), provided the molecule arranges itself in the manner shown.

That the C—C bonds do indeed have this conformation is more easily seen with a model, though the reader may be able to satisfy himself of the fact by a careful consideration of the diagram. (For clarity, the hydrogen atoms have been omitted; they are supposed to be located at the ends of the bonds, two of which radiate from each carbon atom.) All the C—C distances are about 1.54 Å. This form of the cyclohexane molecule is often known as the "chair." It must be admitted that such a chair would not be functionally very efficient (see Fig. 4.6b).

As stereochemists realized half a century ago, another shape might easily be adopted by this molecule. It is shown in Fig. 4.6c, and it is known as the "boat" form (d)—a name the reader may well consider more appropriate than "chair." Inspection of this structure will show it to involve eclipsed conformations about the two C—C bonds lying along the sides of the boat. Since such conformations are now known to impose some strain, the boat form is less stable and is not normally adopted by the molecule

figure 4.6

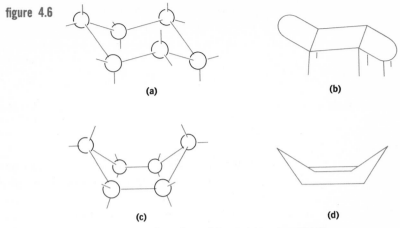

(a)

(b)

(c)

(d)

Chair and boat conformations of the cyclohexane molecule.

of cyclohexane itself. However, some larger molecules are known in which a six-membered ring is *fused* on to other rings whose arrangement is such as to force the cyclohexane-type ring to adopt the boat form.

There is another, even more important, type of ring involving six carbon atoms. This occurs in the molecule of the (*aromatic*) compound benzene, C_6H_6, which has six hydrogen atoms fewer than that of cyclohexane. As we saw on page 52, one way to account for the six extra valences is to suppose there to be alternate single and double bonds round the ring, there being resonance between two possible Kekulé forms. The MO theory covers the situation in a different way. The structure of the benzenoid ring has been carefully determined in benzene itself by both x-ray diffraction on the solid and electron diffraction on the vapor and in many benzene derivatives by x-ray diffraction. The six carbon atoms are arranged in a regular, flat, hexagonal ring; thus all C—C—C angles are 120°.

The C—C distances in benzene are 1.39 Å. The hydrogen atoms are also in the same plane, each lying radially outward at about 1.08 Å from its carbon atom. When some of these hydrogens are replaced by other atoms or groups, there may be slight distortions of the benzenoid ring from exact regularity, but they are not considerable. For instance, in the molecule of naphthalene, $C_{10}H_8$, which consists of two benzenoid rings fused together with

two carbons in common as represented by formula (3), the C—C
distances range from 1.36 to 1.42 Å. Such deviations are of great

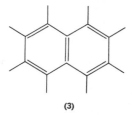

(3)

theoretical interest, but they are unimportant for the purposes of
this book. We shall never be seriously wrong if we regard all
benzenoid rings as being regular hexagons with C—C = 1.4 Å.

One or more of the —CH= units in a benzenoid ring may be replaced by —N= without any notable change in size or shape.
This is one way in which *heterocyclic* molecules are constituted.
Such are pyridine, C_5H_5N, which derives from benzene, or the
various quinolines, C_9H_7N, which derive from naphthalene.

**regularities
among bond
lengths and
covalent-bond
radii**
Presented with a lot of information about the sizes and shapes of
molecules, the chemist naturally looks for evidence of regularities
among these molecular properties. Some of the simplest and most
useful are to be found in bond lengths. These we shall outline in
this section.

The first thing to seek is evidence of *constancy* of bond length.
When two atoms A and B are joined by a covalent bond, is the
A—B distance always the same? The short answer is yes. This
needs a good deal of qualification. We have already seen that the
C—C distance in ethane or cyclohexane is 1.54 Å, while that in
ethylene is 1.34 Å. But the latter molecule has a double bond; we
must restrict ourselves to bonds of the same multiplicity if we
hope to find constancy. There are also some subtler differences.
Careful measurements have shown slight variations in the C—H
bond length: 1.09 in methane, 1.08 in benzene, 1.07 in ethylene,
and 1.06 Å in acetylene. All the same, the rule of constancy is
sufficiently true to be useful, especially when we are merely concerned with broad trends. Single C—C bonds usually have lengths
of 1.54 Å or a little less, and C—H bonds 1.0 Å or a little more.

A second type of regularity might be one of *additivity*. Can we
establish a set of radii, characteristic of each kind of atom, so
that the radii of any two elmeents will add up to the correct dis-

table 4.3 **some covalent radii, Å**

BOND TYPE	C	N	O	F
Single	0.77	0.70	0.66	0.64
Double	(0.67)	(0.60)	(0.55)	...
Triple	(0.60)	(0.55)	(0.50)	...

	P	S	Cl
	1.10	1.04	0.99

	Se	Br
	1.17	1.14

	I
	1.33

tance between these atoms when they are covalently bonded? This would be as if—and we must emphasize the "as if"—the atom were a sphere, with a particular radius for each element, and as if these spheres just came into contact when a bond was formed. The limitations of this view will become evident later, but it can also be useful. One simple way to test the notion of additivity is to compare the related bond lengths A—A, B—B, and A—B. For if the principle holds, and if we represent the characteristic radius by r, then

$$d(A—A) = r_A + r_A$$
$$d(B—B) = r_B + r_B$$
$$d(A—B) = r_A + r_B$$

so that

$$d(A—A) + d(B—B) = 2r_A + 2r_B$$
$$= 2d(A—B)$$

From these equations it is evident that $d(A—B)$ should be the average of the two lengths $d(A—A)$ and $d(B—B)$. Suitable measurements are available for testing this relationship. For instance, we have seen that C—C = 1.54 Å in many compounds and Cl—Cl = 1.98 Å in the chlorine molecule; hence we should expect C—Cl to be $\frac{1}{2}(1.54 + 1.98) = 1.76$ Å. And we duly find C—Cl distances of about this value in many molecules such as those of methyl chloride, CH_3Cl, and carbon tetrachloride, CCl_4.

One set of *covalent radii*, due to Pauling, is shown in Table 4.3. When double or triple bonds are in question, smaller radii are needed; and, for the few elements which normally form multiple bonds, some suitable values are added in parentheses. We shall discuss some failures of the additivity rule in the next section, but a table of this kind is invaluable in enabling us to assess an approximate value for the covalent bond length between two atoms.

bond energies On page 65 we pointed out that the energy D needed to cause a diatomic molecule to dissociate into its two atoms is a measure of the strength of the bond. Zero-point energy slightly complicates the problem, as may also the circumstance that the atoms produced by dissociation of the molecule may not be in their ground states; but any necessary allowances for these can be made. The reaction of splitting a hydrogen molecule into its atoms requires an absorption of 103 kcal of energy per mole, an experimental fact conventionally represented by the following thermochemical equation:

$$H_2 \rightarrow 2H \qquad \Delta H = 103 \text{ kcal}$$

ΔH stands for the increase in the heat content, or enthalpy, of the system when the reaction specified takes place in molar amount. Conversely, when two hydrogen atoms unite to yield a molecule, this same quantity of energy is lost by the system; heat is evolved, as is implied by the negative sign in the reverse equation:

1 $2H \rightarrow H_2 \qquad \Delta H = -103 \text{ kcal}$

Either way, the 103 kcal measures the strength of the H—H bond.

This principle can be applied to more complicated molecules, provided we remember that the energy quantity we need is that for the formation of the molecule *from its atoms*. Hence the normal *heat of formation*, which is understood to apply to the formation of the compound from its elements in the ordinary forms, needs correction. For a simple organic compound this can readily be made as follows. Formation of a mole of methane entails liberation of 18 kcal according to the equation

2 $C(s) + 2H_2 \rightarrow CH_4 \qquad \Delta H = -18 \text{ kcal}$

The carbon is in the solid form of graphite, as is implied by the (s), and the hydrogen is molecular. To convert 12 g of graphite to gaseous, atomic carbon, 170 kcal is needed, or

3 $C(g) \rightarrow C(s)$ $\Delta H = -170$ kcal

Adding equation (3) and twice equation (1) to equation (2), we get

$C(g) + 4H \rightarrow CH_4$ $\Delta H = -170 - 206 - 18 = -394$ kcal

This means, in words, that when the appropriate five atoms combine to constitute a molecule of methane, energy is liberated to the extent of 394 kcal/mole. The process involves simply the creation of four C—H bonds. It is therefore natural to associate one-quarter of this energy, $98\frac{1}{2}$ kcal, with each bond or, conversely, to regard this as the energy needed to break the C—H bond. More precisely, $98\frac{1}{2}$ kcal is the *average* energy needed to break each of the four bonds. There is evidence that, when the bonds are broken in turn, slightly different amounts of energy are absorbed each time; breaking a C—H bond in CH_4 is not quite the same as breaking one in CH_3 or in CH_2. But these are minor complications.

By proceeding in this way, and taking into consideration the thermochemical data for a wide variety of organic compounds, we are able to deduce a set of *bond-energy terms*. These are such that, when we add the terms for each bond in the molecule, the sum is equal to the heat of formation of a mole of the substance from its atoms. The substance is taken to be in gaseous condition to eliminate any small energy effects due to intermolecular forces (see page 93). Some recommended values for the bonds commonly found in biological molecules are listed in Table 4.4. We must stress that the principle of constancy of bond energy, which is implied by this table, does not hold exactly. Indeed, deviations from constancy are commoner and more serious than with bond

table 4.4   **some bond-energy terms, kcal**

C—H	C—C	C≡C	C—O
98	80	145	78

C—N	O—H	N—H	C=O
65	110	93	170

lengths. There are also some systematic causes of large discrepancies to which we shall refer later. All the same, a summation of values from this table often gives a result that is at least roughly correct. For instance, the molecule of ethyl alcohol

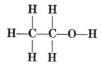

has five C—H bonds and one each of C—C, C—O, and O—H. The energy of formation of this molecule from its atoms should therefore be $5 \times 98 + 80 + 78 + 110 = 758$ kcal/mole. The experimental value is 765 kcal. A small discrepancy like this, in so rough a calculation, need not bother us.

Chemical reactions are always associated with energy changes, and this fact is, literally, of vital importance. For instance, a great part of the energy needed in a technological civilization is still obtained by the combustion of coal. Essentially it derives from the heat liberated in the reaction

$$C(s) + O_2 \rightarrow CO_2 \qquad \Delta H = -94 \text{ kcal}$$

(And when we burn petroleum oils, which are hydrocarbons, much of the heat liberated can be attributed to the combustion of the carbon in the molecules.) Within the living organism, much subtler and more complicated reactions are harnessed to provide the energy needed for bodily warmth or muscular activity.

Now, any chemical reaction can be regarded as the breaking of certain bonds followed by the formation of other bonds. So the net energy release can always be represented as the difference between the energy terms for the bonds on the left-hand side of the equation and the terms for those on the right-hand side.

In the reaction given above, we can suppose that two C—C single bonds are broken for each atom of carbon used, that the bond in an oxygen molecule is also broken, and that two C—O double bonds are formed. On the left-hand side, therefore, we have 2×80 for C—C bonds broken, according to the table, and 120 kcal for dissociating the oxygen molecule. Again taking a value from the table, we have 2×170 kcal for the C=O bond. So the net yield of energy should be $340 - 160 - 120 = 60$ kcal. This is not, in fact, in good agreement with the observed value, but there is reason for supposing the bonds in the carbon dioxide molecule to be abnormally strong, as we shall describe later.

The calculated value can, of course, be brought into formal agreement by raising the C=O bond-energy term for this special case. However, these details are unimportant in the present context. The essential point we are trying to make is that the energies associated with reactions can always be regarded as differences between bond-energy terms. This is a principle of wide applicability.

resonance energy

On page 51 we outlined the VB approximation according to which we may sometimes gain a truer insight into the electronic structure of a molecule by considering it as a blend, or hybrid, of two or more possible formulations. The carbon dioxide molecule, for example, is better represented as a hybrid of formulas (4) to (6) than by any of them singly. When this interpretation is possible, we can correlate it with changes of molecular properties, and especially changes in bond length and bond energies. We shall now describe these observational evidences of resonance. (They can be given an alternative explanation in terms of the MO theory.)

Resonance implies a strengthening of the molecule. It therefore results in—or can be supposed to result in—a shortening of bond lengths and an increase of binding energies. We shall illustrate this viewpoint with bond lengths first.

$$O \equiv C \text{---} O \qquad O = C = O \qquad O \text{---} C \equiv O$$

$$\quad (4) \qquad\qquad\quad (5) \qquad\qquad\quad (6)$$

If formula (4) were adequate by itself, one bond would be single and the other triple. From the radii of Table 4.3 we would expect their lengths to be 1.43 and 1.10 Å, respectively. Formula (6) would lead to expectation in the reverse sense. If (5) were all, the C—O distances would be equal at 1.22 Å. According to the VB theory, the actual bond lengths should be equal, and they should be intermediate between—but less than the average (1.25 Å) of—the three values 1.43, 1.22, and 1.10 Å. Experiment indicates equal lengths of 1.16 Å.

The stabilizing effect of resonance also shows itself in bond energies, and the carbon dioxide molecule illustrates the point, as was suggested in the preceding section. The heat of formation of CO_2 was calculated to be about 60 kcal on the basis of a normal energy term of 170 kcal for each C=O bond. The observed value is greater by some 34 kcal. This excess is known as the *resonance energy;* it can be taken as a measure of the extra stability due to resonance.

These evidences of resonance can be traced in many compounds. A key example is the benzene molecule. As we saw on page 52, this molecule might be represented by a Kekulé-type formula (7). Were this the whole truth, there would be C—C bonds alternately long and short round the ring: 1.54 for the single bonds and 1.34 Å for the double. In fact, the bonds are all of the same length, which

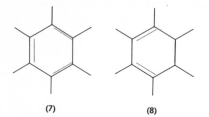

(7)   (8)

is about 1.39 Å. This lies between 1.54 and 1.34, but it is decidedly less than the average. The interpretation, then, is that the molecule is a resonance hybrid between the two Kekulé forms (7) and (8).

The same conclusion follows from a consideration of bonding energy. If (7) alone were valid, the molecule would comprise six C—H, three C—C, and three C=C bonds. Table 4.4 then gives for the energy of formation of gaseous benzene from its atoms:

$$6 \times 98 + 3 \times 80 + 3 \times 145 = 1{,}263 \text{ kcal/mole}$$

The experimental value is 1,307 kcal, which is greater by 44 kcal. This is the resonance energy measuring the enhanced stability of the benzene molecule. Similar considerations can be applied to both bond lengths and bond energies in all aromatic compounds, and indeed in many other compounds of all types.

We must not fail to emphasize the arbitrary nature of the resonance concept. That bond lengths are found to be shortened, and energies of formation increased, are factual evidence of enhanced stability. They can be interpreted in VB terms, but they do not *prove* that resonance is occurring. Resonance—and the VB method generally—constitutes one very useful approximation to the exact wave-mechanical description of a molecule. There is the alternative MO approximation (see page 44), which interprets the facts in a different way. If the exact wave-mechanical treatment of a moderate-sized molecule were not impossibly difficult, we should not need either approximation. However, provided we recognize its limitations, there is no objection to discussing a wide range of chemical observations in terms of resonance. For chemists, who have long been accustomed to think of the atoms in molecules as being held together by bonds, this VB method seems especially convenient.

resonance and the peptide linkage

As we stated on page 75, the six atoms of the peptide group (9) are coplanar, or very nearly so. This fact has proved to be of the greatest significance in helping us to understand the structures of certain proteins. Since it can be neatly interpreted in terms of resonance theory, we may discuss the problem here. The central C—N bond of the group—the peptide linkage—is always found to be shorter than one would expect for the formally single bond appearing in bond diagram (9). The other C—N bond shown has a normal length of about 1.47 Å; the peptide bond, about 1.33 Å. In VB terminology this shortening implies that the bond has some double-bond character, or that there is resonance involving some contribution from a form like (10) with a double C—N bond.

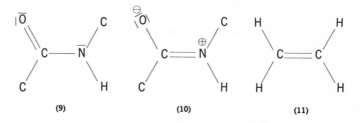

(9)   (10)   (11)

This has a stereochemical consequence, for we have already seen that the four atoms attached to a double-bonded pair of carbon atoms—as in ethylene (11)—tend to be coplanar. The similar situation in (10) will have a similar result around the peptide linkage. In other words, there will be no free rotation about the peptide linkage (see page 48).

odd molecules and free radicals

A remarkable fact which was noticed at an early stage in the development of electronic theories of valence is that nearly all stable molecules contain an even number of electrons. This we can now appreciate as a consequence of the stability of electron groupings in which a set of orbitals is completely filled, with a pair of electrons in each orbital. Because this rule of even numbers is so widely obeyed, cases where it is broken—where a well-characterized molecule possesses an odd number of electrons—are the more remarkable. Among simple substances about half a dozen of these "odd molecules" are known. Important examples are nitric oxide, NO, nitrogen dioxide, NO_2, chlorine dioxide, ClO_2, and triphenylmethyl, $C(C_6H_5)_3$. (The last formula is meant to cover a large number of its derivatives as well—i.e., compounds in whose molecules some of the hydrogen atoms are replaced by other groups, such as the nitro group.)

All these substances possess the unusual property of *paramagnetism*. Nearly all materials are *diamagnetic*, which means that a bar-shaped piece of the material, if supported on a pivot in a magnetic field, tends to orient itself so that its length lies at right angles to the field. This effect is a very weak one, and a highly sensitive apparatus is needed to measure it. A bar-shaped piece of a *paramagnetic* substance, on the other hand, tends to orient itself parallel to the direction of the field. Though decidedly stronger than diamagnetism, this effect is still relatively weak; and both are many times weaker than the familiar behavior of *ferromagnetic* substances such as iron. Paramagnetism is associated with the presence in the material of *unpaired electrons;* indeed, a measurement of the magnitude of the effect serves as a guide to the number of unpaired electrons per molecule.

All compounds with odd molecules are therefore paramagnetic. In addition, they are almost always colored and chemically reactive. Nitric oxide is exceptional in being colorless and moderately stable, but NO_2 tends to dimerize to yield N_2O_4, triphenylmethyl tends to dimerize to yield hexamethylethane, $C_2(CH_3)_6$, and ClO_2 is explosive.

Since these molecules contain odd numbers of electrons, we obviously cannot write for them electronic formulas which obey the ordinary rules (page 35), with completed octets and electron-pair bonds. We shall illustrate the difficulty, and sketch a possible way out of it, by detailed reference to the NO molecule. Here we start with eleven valence electrons, five in the outer shell of the nitrogen atom and six in oxygen. By following the conventional rules as far as we can, we can easily construct an imperfect electronic formula such as (12). This uses the proper number of electrons and has the completed octet around the oxygen atom; but the nitrogen atom has a group of only seven electrons, and the formula is to this extent unsatisfactory.

$$\overset{\bullet}{N} = \overset{\backslash}{O}_{\diagup} \qquad \diagup \overset{}{N} = \overset{\bullet}{O}_{\diagup}$$

(12)   (13)

We can similarly construct formula (13), in which the oxygen atom now has only the septet of electrons, so that this formula also is unsatisfactory. Certain other formulas which are even less satisfying can be contrived. Yet nitric oxide is a reasonably stable compound. Various explanations of this apparent anomaly can be offered. The simplest, for a chemist, is one based on the VB approximation. We suppose that the actual molecule of NO is a resonance hybrid of forms corresponding to (12) and (13) and that the resonance energy is sufficient to offset the energetic disadvantage of the odd electron in the septet. For a useful amount of resonance energy it is essential that the two forms be of nearly equal energy. This may be so because oxygen and nitrogen are sufficiently similar elements, so that it will not make much difference whether the odd electron is on one atom or the other.

We might seek some confirmation of this resonance explanation by considering the bond length, which is 1.15 Å. However, this is about normal for a double bond between nitrogen and oxygen. So the resonance between (12) and (13) has not produced appreciable shortening of the bond, but this may be because it has to compete with the destabilizing influences of the unsatisfactory contributory forms.

The reader should check the similar formulation of the NO_2 molecule for himself. He should have no difficulty in writing four forms of the type (14), and resonance may be presumed to operate between these four. As formula (14) suggests, this molecule is bent, with the O—N—O angle about 134° and the two equal N—O distances about 1.19 Å.

(14)

Substances that have odd molecules but are stable enough to be isolated are uncommon. We now recognize, however, that odd molecules are very common as transient entities during chemical reactions. Their very instability renders them valuable as reactive intermediaries. In this context they are usually referred to as *free radicals*. Simple examples are the neutral atoms H˙ and Cl˙, the methyl radical ˙CH₃, and the hydroxyl radical ˙OH. To each of these formulas the dot has been added to emphasize the presence of the odd electron. Such radicals play an essential role in *chain reactions*. A very simple example of a chain reaction is the union of hydrogen and chlorine under the influence of light. In the dark, the reaction $H_2 + Cl_2 \rightarrow 2HCl$ occurs only very slowly; on exposure to light, the mixture reacts very rapidly and is likely to explode. The interpretation was given by the German physical chemist Walther Nernst (1864–1941). Under the influence of light, provided it is of suitable wavelength, chlorine dissociates into two chlorine atoms:

Cl_2 + light energy → $2Cl˙$

These Cl˙ free radicals are much more reactive than Cl_2 molecules. When one of them collides with a hydrogen molecule, reaction occurs, yielding a hydrogen atom (i.e., another free radical)

$Cl˙ + H_2 \rightarrow HCl + H˙$

which then reacts with a chlorine molecule,

$H˙ + Cl_2 \rightarrow HCl + Cl˙$

producing a second chlorine radical. Thus the cycle repeats itself, in principle, indefinitely. So a single initial act, caused by absorption of light, gives rise to a large number of acts of combination between H_2 and Cl_2. This is a chain reaction.

Free radicals can be produced in other ways, and in particular by suitable chemical reagents; and many important reactions occur by a chain mechanism. The manufacture of polymeric substances, such as polyethylene and synthetic rubber, depends on chain reactions. Many biological reactions also involve chains, though the free radicals concerned will usually be more complex than the simple entities mentioned here.

the oxygen molecule

In the oxygen molecule we have 2×6 valence electrons to account for. By following the usual rules, we have no difficulty in arriving at what seems to be a satisfactory electronic formula (15). But consideration of the properties of oxygen shows this formula to be unacceptable. In the first place, molecular oxygen is paramagnetic; the molecule must therefore possess unpaired electrons, which do not appear in (15). Again, the spectrum is not consistent with this formula. Furthermore, the chemical reactivity of oxygen is much greater than such a formula would lead us to expect.

$$\langle O \!=\! O \rangle \qquad |\dot{\underline{O}} \!-\! \overline{O}| \qquad |\overline{O} \!-\! \dot{\underline{O}}|$$

(15)   (16)   (17)

The anomalous behavior of oxygen can be explained by supposing the molecule to be a "double odd molecule" (or a "biradical"), such as indicated by formula (16). The disadvantage that neither atom in (16) has a complete octet of electrons is compensated because resonance can occur with the equivalent form (17). The observed interatomic distance is 1.207 Å, which is substantially greater than 1.10 Å, the sum of the covalent radii for double-bonded oxygen atoms.

Though the facts undoubtedly require us to reject formula (15), we must confess that this is surprising. There must be little to choose between (15) on the one hand and (16) with (17) on the other. Some subtle effect, which theory can roughly assess, makes the latter slightly more stable. Whatever the underlying causes, the consequences are, literally, of vital importance. Most higher organisms depend for their energy upon the combustion of carbon compounds with the oxygen of the atmosphere. That energy depends, therefore, on the presence of free oxygen in the environment (see Chap. 6). Because of its reactivity, molecular oxygen combines with other elements, and it is not normally found free in the universe. Hence, for the existence of animal life as we know it, a necessary prerequisite is a mechanism for producing free oxygen, and this is provided by the chlorophyll of green plants.

The absorption of oxygen by animal life depends on hemoglobin, which rapidly combines with molecular oxygen and then conveys it to the sites where it can enter the sequence of oxidation reactions. Hemoglobin, like oxygen, is paramagnetic; but when the two combine, the resulting oxyhemoglobin is diamagnetic. The unpaired electrons on each reactant become paired in the product.

This cannot be the only factor favorable to the combination; for the carbon monoxide molecule, CO, combines even more readily with hemoglobin (which helps to explain its poisonous propensities). Carbon monoxide is diamagnetic, and hence the molecule must be without unpaired electrons. With $4 + 6 = 10$ electrons to accommodate, the most obvious formula is (18). Examination of this formula will show that its atoms carry the formal charges indicated. They would produce a high dipole moment. In fact, the

$$\overset{\ominus}{|C} \equiv \overset{\oplus}{O|} \qquad |C = \overset{\diagdown}{O} \qquad \overset{\oplus}{|C} \overline{} \overset{\ominus}{\underline{O}|}$$

$$\text{(18)} \qquad\qquad \text{(19)} \qquad\qquad \text{(20)}$$

moment of carbon monoxide is very small ($\sim$0.1 D). This may be explained by supposing that the molecule is really a resonance hybrid between (18) and some other forms, one (at least) of which must have a dipole moment in the opposite direction. Two possibilities are represented in formulas (19) and (20), in which, however, the carbon atom fails to achieve an octet. Formula (20) has its polarity in the sense contrary to that of (18). None of these formulas embodies any unpaired electrons. It is a condition for resonance that all contributory forms must have the same number of unpaired spins—in the case of CO, zero.

5

other interatomic forces and the hydrogen bond

electrovalence
and covalence

In Chap. 2 we described two important types of forces that may join atoms together. They are electrovalence and covalence. The former involves the transfer of one or more electrons from one atom to another. By the transfer, the atoms become positively and negatively charged ions, which are sometimes said to be joined by an ionic bond. Although the force is a strong one, it is not well described by the word "bond," since all the oppositely charged ions attract one another. There is a general, overall attraction, and the ions arrange themselves as conditions permit (see page 33).

The covalent type of force, on the other hand, corresponds more closely to the notion of a bond linking a particular pair of atoms. Formally, this is generally attributable to the sharing of a pair of electrons by the two bonded atoms. In its apparently quite different way this also leads to a strong force of attraction. The force is one that plays an all-important role in building the molecules with which we are concerned in this book.

Our objects in the present chapter are to compare electrovalence and covalence, to consider whether they are related to one another, and to ask if—and how far—other types of force are important in regulating the influences of atoms or molecules upon each other.

At first sight, electrovalence and covalence seem quite different. The one is an electrostatic attraction resulting from a transfer of electrons, while the other depends on a subtler wave-mechanical effect, not recognized in classical physics, connected with the sharing of electron pairs. There is also an important difference in the way these two forces die away with distance. Electrovalence follows the inverse-square law: if we double the distance between the ions, the force diminishes to one-quarter. The covalent force diminishes much more rapidly. It is emphatically a short-range force, very strong between a pair of atoms at, or near, the normal bonded distance, but almost negligible when the bond is stretched beyond double that distance. Interionic forces, though diminished, are still appreciable at much greater distances. In this respect they are unique among interatomic forces—a fact which has some interesting consequences—notably in the behavior of ions as very unorthodox solutes.

Despite the formal difference, current opinion regards pure electrovalence and pure covalence as ideal types: actual bonds are usually regarded as intermediate in character—part covalence, part electrovalence. We can illustrate this in an elementary way by considering the bonding in the gaseous hydrogen chloride molecule, HCl. This molecule is dipolar; it has a dipole moment of about 1.0 D, and this is certainly in the sense that the hydrogen atom carries some net positive charge and the chlorine some negative charge. To signify this polarity, we can represent the molecule as $\overset{\delta+}{H}$—$\overset{\delta-}{Cl}$, implying that the effective charges are less than the full electronic charge (see page 69). We can "explain" this by stating that chlorine is more electronegative than hydrogen, so that the shared electron pair is drawn some way from the hydrogen atom toward the chlorine.

A complementary "explanation" adopts VB terminology: the actual molecule is to be regarded as a resonance hybrid of a hypothetical, purely covalent form H—Cl with no dipole moment and a hypothetical, purely ionic form H^+Cl^- which would have a large dipole moment. The former makes the major contribution to the hybrid, so that the actual molecule has about one-sixth of the dipole moment ($\sim$6 D) expected for H^+Cl^-.

It is important not to suppose that some of the hydrogen chloride molecules are ionic and some not. According to the basic principles of VB theory, all the molecules are the same, but they are intermediate in character between the two extreme forms. Of course, when hydrogen chloride is dissolved in water, it ionizes as hydrochloric acid; but that is another matter, which we discuss briefly on page 137.

From the point of view described above, any bond can be regarded as having covalent and electrovalent contributions and therefore as being of intermediate character. However, it turns out that in most cases the character is predominantly of one kind or the other. For our purposes, the distinction between electrovalence and covalence is a valid and useful one. We can regard the bonds between carbon, hydrogen, oxygen, and nitrogen atoms in all ordinary organic molecules as substantially covalent and the forces between the ions of a salt as simply electrovalent. Cases where there is something like a 50:50 covalent/ionic contribution to a bond are rare.

other types of force between atoms

Whether we regard electrovalence and covalence as two distinct interactions between atoms or whether we adopt a more sophisticated attitude toward them, these forces are undoubtedly of prime importance in an elementary account of molecules. We may now ask if other types of interaction ought to be considered. The answer is yes, and that there are several of them. With one exception, they are relatively weak forces. Energy amounting to about 10^2 kcal/mole is required to break a typical covalent bond (page 81); and while the cohesion of ionic compounds needs assessing on a different basis, the amounts of energy involved are similar. Most of the forces we are to describe in this section have energies of about 10 kcal or less; they are ten or twenty times weaker. Nevertheless, they play significant roles in molecular biology.

The above exception, though not important in biology, should be mentioned. The atoms in most *metals* are held together very strongly indeed, though the forces doing this holding cannot be regarded as electrovalent or covalent. All metals are elements whose atoms have a small number of electrons loosely held around an atomic core. Iron has two such electrons, whereas the 24 electrons of the core are more strongly bound—23 of them much more strongly.

A rough, but useful, way to picture such a metal is to suppose it to consist of a regular, closely packed arrangement of spherical metal ions (Fe^{++} in the case of iron) embedded in a "cement" of electrons. These electrons—two contributed by each iron atom— are held in common by the whole of the metal. The word "cement" represents a useful analogy in so far as these electrons bind the atoms together very firmly (iron has a very high melting point).

It is misleading if it suggests fixity of the electrons, which are in fact free to move easily through the whole mass of metal, thus accounting for several properties characteristic of metals, notably the high electrical conductivity.

That weakly attractive forces may operate between ordinary molecules is suggested by many considerations. One piece of evidence is the deviation of gases from ideal behavior. The ideal gas law, $PV = RT$, can be deduced on the assumption that the molecules are infinitely small (i.e., point particles) and exert no attraction upon one another. When the pressure is high or the temperature low—or under any conditions if the measurements of pressure and volume are very accurate—all gases deviate more or less from the exact requirements of the law, $PV = RT$ per mole.

These deviations imply that the two assumptions are not perfectly valid. They can be allowed for by using more sophisticated assumptions, which will lead to a more complicated equation. The most famous such equation is that of the Dutch physicist Johannes Diderik van der Waals (1837–1923)

$$(P + a/V^2)(V - b) = RT$$

The a/V^2 term allows for the attraction between the molecules; the b term allows for the fact that they occupy an appreciable volume. Here we are concerned with the attractive forces. They occur in all gases. In general they are the more important, the larger the molecule; but they are detectable even with small and simple molecules like those of the inert gases.

One type of attraction additional to the ordinary valence forces occurs between an ion and a polar molecule. When such a molecule finds itself near an ion, it will tend to orient itself in such a direction that its poles are in line with the ion, with due regard to sign. For instance, a water molecule near a positive ion such as Na^+ will be at a lower state of potential energy if oriented with its oxygen atom, which carries a partial negative charge, toward the ion and its hydrogen atoms, which carry partial positive charges, away from it, as suggested in Fig. 5.1a. In this position, the $+$ charge on the sodium ion and the two $\delta-$ charges on the oxygen atom will attract one another, while the $+$ charge on the ion will repel the two $\delta+$ charges on the hydrogens. But the forces of attraction and repulsion will be unequal. According to the inverse-square law, the attraction will exceed the repulsion because the unlike set of charges are closer together than the like set.

This type of attraction is known as the *ion-dipole force*. Though usually weaker than a covalent bond, it is of considerable strength. Owing to its small size, an isolated ion has a very intense electrostatic field. This force is a principal cause of the hydration of ions in solution (see page 137), and it is likely to produce notable effects whenever ions are close to polar molecules. Of course, it is not important in connection with the behavior of ordinary gases, since they do not contain ions.

A similar, though weaker, force will operate even when the molecule has zero dipole moment (e.g., benzene or iodine). The intense field of the ion will disturb the electronic arrangement of any molecule that comes close to it. If the ion is a positive one, the electrons of the molecule will be drawn a little toward the ion and the atomic nulcei will be repelled. In consequence the molecule will now have an *induced dipole* even if it is inherently nonpolar. This induced moment is necessarily in the sense required to yield a net attraction, since we again have the situation suggested in Fig. 5.1a. This is known as the *ion-induced-dipole force*.

There is also a *dipole-dipole force*. Polar molecules will tend to orient themselves when near other polar molecules. Two possible types of mutual orientation are shown in Fig. 5.1b and c; (b) involves only two molecules, but (c) might involve the "lining up" of several. In either case a net attraction results, as can be easily deduced from considerations of the kind used above in connection with the ion-dipole interaction. The attraction is weak. Still weaker is the corresponding *dipole-induced-dipole force*, which obtains between a polar molecule and its nonpolar neighbors.

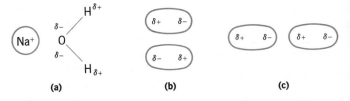

(a)   (b)   (c)

Modes of approach leading to an electrostatic attraction between (a) an ion and a polar (water) molecule, and (b) two polar molecules.

Our list of intermolecular forces is still not complete. This we can infer from the consideration that even nonpolar molecules, such as H_2 or N_2 or those of the inert gases, attract one another. Evidence for this attraction lies in the fact that these gases deviate from ideal behavior and ultimately condense to liquids when sufficiently cooled and/or compressed. A wave-mechanical explanation of such a force was discovered by Fritz London, a German-born chemist, in 1930. Here we can offer only a pictorial interpretation as follows: Even a nonpolar molecule can be supposed to have a transient polarity. At a given instant of time, the electrons might be so disposed as temporarily to displace the center of negative charge away from the center of positive charge. In a hydrogen molecule, for example, the pair of electrons is shared equally between the two nuclei when considered over any observable period of time. But at some single instant of time they might lie closer to one nucleus than to the other, so that a temporary dipole moment would result. Such a temporary dipole would induce a dipole moment in any neighboring molecule. Similarly, the neighboring molecule might induce a temporary moment in the first one. Theory shows that these mutual effects will tend to get into phase with one another, so as to lead to a net attraction, even though the dipole moments of the molecules are zero when averaged over an appreciable period of time. This type of attraction, which is very weak, is known as the *dispersion force*.

There is still one more intermolecular force. This is the *hydrogen bond*, which is especially important and which we shall therefore describe in some detail in a later section. Meantime, it is convenient to summarize the general picture we have been sketching. The picture becomes a little simpler if we concentrate attention on neutral molecules, and so can disregard forces involving ions. Weak forces of attraction exist between all molecules. These forces are of short range; they are appreciable only when the molecules are close together. In all cases the dispersion force makes its contribution. In addition, the other forces will act where appropriate. If one of the molecules is dipolar, there will be a dipole-induced-dipole contribution; if both are dipolar, there will be contributions from both this and from the dipole-dipole force. Hydrogen bonding may operate as well.

The total attraction between two molecules, made up of contributions from some, or all, of these components, is often termed the *van der Waals force*, because it reveals itself to observation in the a/V^2 term of the celebrated equation. Many other effects can also be attributed to it.

repulsive forces between molecules

So far we have been considering attractive forces between atoms and molecules, but we have said nothing explicitly about repulsive forces. These latter must obviously exist; for if they did not, unopposed attraction would cause the atoms in a molecule to collapse into a single atom or the molecules in any piece of matter to coalesce into a single molecule. The part played by repulsive forces was implied in our discussion (pages 61 to 69) of the potential-energy diagram for a diatomic molecule.

An attractive force, which is mainly covalent in nature in a molecule such as H_2, HCl, or Cl_2, draws the atoms together, the attraction increasing rapidly with decreasing distance. However, when the distance becomes small enough, a repulsive force develops; this also increases with decreasing distance, and it does so much more rapidly than the attraction does. The difference in the way the forces vary with internuclear distance means that there must be a particular distance d_e at which the two forces just balance. This corresponds to the most stable situation, with lowest potential energy, and—as the subscript signifies—to an equilibrium. (In fact, the principle of zero-point energy requires there to be always a certain amount of vibration on either side of the equilibrium point.)

In the same way, when two molecules are close together, they will attract each other—though less strongly—by the various types of forces we described in the preceding section. They will tend to move closer together until some of the atoms of one molecule come within range of the repulsive forces from some atoms of the other. A similar state of balance will result.

A general understanding of these repulsive forces is easy to come by. The outer parts of all atoms consist of electrons. As the atoms come closer together, their outer electrons will be forced into close proximity and, since negatively charged bodies repel one another, a repulsive force will develop rapidly. There is one exception. If the electrons can enter molecular orbitals—a pair with opposite spins in each orbital—then a covalent bond is formed, and this bond overrides the repulsion until the atoms are much closer together. We then say that a bond has been formed between the two atoms. In all other circumstances the repulsion keeps the non-bonded atoms well apart. Repulsive force between the positively charged atomic nuclei also makes a contribution.

The closest possible approach of atoms which are not directly bonded to one another is what principally concerns us in this section. We often represent molecules by models consisting of balls. Two such balls can be brought toward each other without experiencing any resistance until their surfaces make contact. This is a poor imitation of an atom, nearly all of whose volume consists of electrons. The electron density, measured by ψ^2 (see page 28), dies away gradually, and it does not stop suddenly at a boundary surface.

Nevertheless, just because repulsive forces are negligible at considerable distances from the center of the atom and build up sharply as the distance diminishes past a certain value, the notion of a distinct surface has a rough validity. Suppose we are trying to pack two methane molecules, CH_4, together. When their separation is such that the centers of the hydrogen atoms belonging to different molecules are more than, say, 2.4 Å apart, there will be little repulsion; but, when the centers of approaching hydrogen atoms are forced just a little closer (say, to within 2.2 Å), a large repulsion will operate. Thus, surprisingly, it is not too inexact to think of the hydrogen atoms as having "surfaces" about 1.2 Å from their central nuclei and to regard these surfaces as coming into some sort of "contact" (with the onset of severe repulsion) when the centers of nonbonded atoms come within 2.4 Å of each other.

On the other hand, when two hydrogen atoms can put their electrons into a common molecular orbital, forming a covalent bond, a much stronger force of attraction obtains; the atoms can then come much closer together ($\sim$0.74 Å between their centers) before the repulsive force wins the upper hand. This situation must be clearly distinguished from the one we are considering in this section.

When the structure of a crystal is elucidated with x-rays, we discover how the atoms are situated with respect to each other within the molecule; but we also learn how closely the atoms of contiguous molecules can approach. By surveying the great mass of informa-

table 5.1   **some van der Waals radii, Å**

H	N	O	F
1.2	1.5	1.4	1.35
	P	S	Cl
	1.9	1.85	1.8
			Br
			1.95
Methyl group			
(—CH₃)		I	
2.0		2.15	

tion now available on crystal structures, we can deduce the minimum distances that must exist between nonbonded atoms, and particularly between atoms of different molecules. We find that this minimum distance is roughly constant for two atoms of particular kinds. We can construct a table of radii for the elements such that the sum of the respective radii for two atoms will equal their minimum separation. They are known as *van der Waals radii* because they are related to the term b in van der Waals' equation (page 94).

Pauling drew up a table of these radii, and some of his values are listed in Table 5.1. We notice that the radii are about twice the corresponding covalent bond radii, that they decrease with atomic number within any one period, but that they increase within any one group of the periodic table.

At first sight the reader may be surprised that we give no value for carbon. This is because a "naked" carbon atom rarely protrudes from a molecule; external contact is more likely to be made via the hydrogen atoms bonded to it. So the table carries an effective van der Waals radius for the methyl group. The carbon atoms of methyl groups belonging to different molecules rarely come much closer to each other than 4 Å, though somewhat closer approaches may occur provided that the hydrogen atoms of one methyl group can mesh into the gaps between the hydrogens of the other.

One other contact distance may be mentioned. Aromatic molecules are often packed into crystals with their benzenoid rings parallel, though never with the atoms of one molecule exactly

superposed on those of the next. It is then found that the minimum
distance perpendicularly between the planes of these rings is
about $3\frac{1}{2}$ Å.

The simple concept of the fixed van der Waals radius may not
apply when the two atoms are part of the same molecule. For
instance, the radius for chlorine given in Table 5.1 would pro-
hibit two nonbonded atoms from being closer together than about
3.6 Å. But in the carbon tetrachloride molecule, CCl_4, which has
a regular tetrahedral structure with C—Cl = 1.76 Å, pairs of
chlorine atoms are separated by only $\sqrt{8/3} \times 1.76 = 2.86$ Å.

One might try to evade this difficulty by arguing that the atoms
have no choice: the tetrahedral structure forces pairs of chlorine
atoms into this close proximity; it is a price the molecule has to
pay in return for being able to form four strong C—Cl bonds.
However, there is a molecule CH_2Cl_2 in which two of the chlorines
are replaced by two much smaller hydrogen atoms. The supposed
stress caused by the two close chlorine atoms could be avoided
here if the Cl—C—Cl angle were to open up considerably. In
fact, this happens only to a minor extent. The angle increases by
about $2\frac{1}{2}°$ from the tetrahedral value, so that the chlorine atoms
are still only 2.9 Å apart, which is well below the formal require-
ment of 3.6 Å. We may suppose that the full van der Waals radius
is effective only in directions out from the C—Cl bond. In directions lateral to the bond, the electron density is less extensive.

the validity of molecular models

Models are extremely useful in enabling us to form an idea of a
molecule and its behavior. Properly they should be solid, three-
dimensional objects. In books and diagrams we have to restrict
ourselves to two dimensions. There is, of course, the possibility
of stereoscopy; but this is expensive, and it is troublesome to the
reader. Failing that, we may try to suggest the third dimension
either by photographing actual solid models or by giving some
form of perspective to our line drawings. The latter procedure is
usually more satisfactory.

Molecular models often make use of plastic balls, with different
colors to represent atoms of different elements. The balls are
drilled with suitably disposed holes, into which thin rods may be
fitted to represent valence bonds. In this way ball-and-stick
models can be constructed, and many of the drawings used in

this book can be regarded as rough sketches of such models. Indeed, at a primitive level all structural formulas (such as those on pages 7, 9, and 75) are conventional representations of simplified molecular models. At this point, we may usefully consider the validity of models.

As we have stated before, no one has ever seen a molecule. A molecule is in a sense a hypothetical notion which serves to account for certain observable properties of the material. Originally these were the chemical properties mainly, but now we have to account for a wider range of properties such as the spectrum or the x-ray diffraction pattern. So our idea of the molecule has become more sophisticated; it involves many parameters which can be given numerical values, as we saw in Chap. 4.

As an example, we shall take the water molecule and consider what sort of mental picture it suggests in the light of elementary theory and our knowledge of its properties. There is an oxygen nucleus of mass 16 carrying a positive charge of 8 units. Rather less than 1 Å away are two hydrogen nuclei, each of unit mass and unit positive charge. These hydrogen nuclei subtend an angle of about 105° at the oxygen. The angle and the distances are not fixed, for the molecule is always vibrating. The 10 positive charges on the three nuclei are balanced by 10 electrons, which are much lighter than the nuclei.

Except when we wish to remove one of them, these electrons are not to be regarded simply as particles, but rather as a distribution of electron density. Near the oxygen nucleus, with its relatively high charge, there is a high electron density, which tends to diminish as we move outward. Though there is no sharp boundary to the atom, the electron density has fallen to a low value at 1.4 Å, the van der Waals radius of oxygen. In the water molecule, however, the density does not fall off uniformly in all directions. The presence of the protons (hydrogen nuclei) produces a minor, local condensation of electrons near each; and the covalent bonding must correspond to some enhancement of electron density between the oxygen nucleus and each proton, though any such enhancement is probably slight. This nonuniform distribution of electrons, as well as the arrangement of the positive nuclei, results in an overall electrical polarity measurable as a dipole moment.

Now let us contrast this mental picture with a conventional ball-and-stick model consisting of three balls linked by two sticks. If the usual color code were followed, the oxygen atom would consist of a blue ball about one inch in diameter. Two holes would be drilled in the ball to take sticks radiating at about the correct angle. These sticks would fit into holes in the two white balls, perhaps somewhat less in diameter, which represent the hydrogen atoms. If a scale model were intended, the sticks would be cut to such a length that the centers of the blue and white balls would be an appropriate distance apart. A scale of 2 in. to the Å would be typical.

A sketch of such a model is shown in Fig. 5.2a. Its imperfections are many and manifest. The balls are much too large to represent the atomic nuclei in proportion, but too small to represent the whole atom. The bonding electrons are overemphasized by the rigid sticks, while the other electrons are ignored. For instance, taken at their face value, such models would allow two or more molecules to be packed much more closely together—as is sketched in Fig. 5.2b—than corresponds to the van der Waals radii. They are unrealistic in respect of the extension of electron density.

From this point of view the alternative of Fig. 5.2c is better. It shows the electron distribution around the oxygen as spherical with a radius scaled to 1.4 Å. The small distortion caused by the hydrogen atoms is harder to represent, but it may perhaps be suggested by slightly extending the "boundary" in the region of each. (The outcome has been described as an "oxygen atom with mumps.") Ingenious plastic models have been invented to yield

figure 5.2

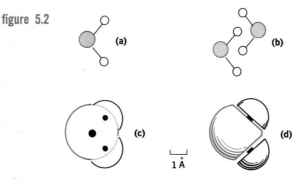

Representations of the water molecule.

this sort of effect, those of H. A. Stuart being especially popular. They consist of nonspherical pieces of material and have suitably disposed holes and pegs, so that, when plugged together, their centers are in the correct relative positions for covalent bonding, while their surfaces correspond to the correct van der Waals radii. Figure 5.2d is intended to show the result.

Stuart-type models are most useful when we wish to study the possible ways in which molecules can be packed together without infringing the van der Waals radii of their atoms. All types of model are misleading in that they cannot easily convey the polarity of a molecule, the fact of its vibrations, or the possibility that it may undergo considerable distortion when other factors make this energetically worthwhile.

Despite their imperfections, ball-and-stick models are very useful. They are cheap and easy to make, and they are easy to represent in diagrams, a circumstance which renders them especially valuable to the author of a book. Just because the outer electron density is omitted, we can see the skeleton of the molecule the more clearly. They will not seriously mislead the reader so long as he remembers their limitations, and, in particular, so long as he mentally adds on the appropriate van der Waals radius to each atom when molecular contacts are in question.

the hydrogen bond Hydrogen has a covalence of unity; indeed, the univalence of hydrogen was a basic principle in classical chemistry. Great interest therefore attached to the discovery of cases where a single hydrogen was linked to two other atoms—where its apparent valence was 2. One example is particularly striking and well established, though it is not typical: the bifluoride anion, HF_2^-, which occurs in a number of salts. This ion was suspected to have its three atoms arranged as F---H---F, a suspicion which has been amply confirmed by more recent work. The hydrogen atom certainly holds two fluorines together. More typical is a situation often found when the crystal structures of hydroxylic compounds are elucidated by x-ray analysis. It is found that two oxygen atoms of different molecules are situated at a distance apart decidedly less than 2.8 Å, the sum of their van der Waals radii. Distances found in various crystalline compounds range down to about 2.4 Å, with a great number of examples between

2.75 and 2.45 Å. A notable example is ice, though its O . . . O distance is not particularly short, being 2.76 Å.

Now such a distance is too short for an ordinary nonbonded contact, and it is much too long for a direct covalence, which would require only about 1.4 Å between the atoms. (The minimum van der Waals separation of two nonbonded oxygen atoms should be 2.8 Å; but if one of the oxygens carries a hydrogen atom, the minimum nonbonded distance in that direction must be increased to about 3.2 Å to allow room for the hydrogen. So O . . . O distances *greater* than 2.8 Å may imply a hydrogen bond when we know for certain that a hydrogen atom is interposed.) Though hydrogen atoms do not show up well in x-ray crystal-structure analysis, it was reasonable to suppose that one lay between such a pair of neighboring oxygen atoms, which were in fact somehow linked by the hydrogen. This has been confirmed, both by meticulous x-ray analysis in a few cases, and—where the method has been applied—by neutron diffraction, which is better adapted for locating hydrogen atoms.

In a much more general way, chemists had long realized that hydroxylic compounds show anomalous properties. Water shows these anomalies in an extreme form, and we shall discuss it at some length in Chap. 6, but alcohols, phenols, and carboxylic acids are all anomalous in some degree. It became accepted chemical doctrine that this behavior could be attributed to *molecular association*, which means a tendency for the molecules to combine together. Also, since the anomalous behavior disappears when the hydrogen atom of the hydroxyl group is replaced by a methyl group, it was inferred that the association occurs via the hydrogen atom in a manner which was subsequently found to occur in crystals, as we have just described.

This linking of two atoms via a hydrogen has come to be known as *hydrogen bonding*. Though rather a weak force, it is extremely important throughout chemistry and biochemistry. We shall discuss its incidence, its properties, and its nature.

Hydrogen bonding may occur between two molecules when one of them includes a group —X—H and the other a group —Y. (The extra bonds are meant to indicate attachment of X and Y to the rest of their respective molecules.) X and Y must be highly electronegative (see page 69), and serious hydrogen bonding is largely restricted to the three most electronegative elements: fluorine, oxygen, and nitrogen. For example, when two molecules of an alcohol (which we can generalize as ROH) approach one another in a suitable presentation, they may set up a hydrogen bond thus:

$$H—O \quad H—O \rightarrow H—O\text{-}\text{-}\text{-}H—O$$
$$\underset{R}{|} + \underset{R}{|} \quad \underset{R}{|} \quad \underset{R}{|}$$

This shows an association to yield a double molecule, but a third or a fourth molecule could possibly join on. Molecules containing the >NH group can also form hydrogen bonds; an example would be the union of an imide, R_2NH, with a ketone, R_2CO:

$$R_2N—H\text{-}\text{-}\text{-}O{=}CR_2$$

We normally represent the hydrogen bond by the broken line, and we can do this without, at this stage, committing ourselves to any theory of how the attractive force originates.

Given molecules with suitable —X—H and —Y groups, hydrogen bonding is common, and we shall discuss some important consequences later. When molecules of the appropriate kind come together in the solid state, they are very "clever" in arranging themselves to form a maximum number of hydrogen bonds. The sugars are an example: glucose (see page 10) has a molecule with five hydroxyl groups, and in the crystal they are all able to join in a system of hydrogen bonds with neighboring molecules. The splendid crystals formed by ordinary cane sugar can be partly attributed to extensive hydrogen bonding.

We now summarize some properties of hydrogen bonds. The binding is relatively weak. Whereas the energy needed to break a typical covalent bond lies in the range 50 to 100 kcal/mole, that needed for hydrogen bonds is about 5 kcal. Actual values range from 2 or 3 kcal for very weak bonds up to 8 to 12 kcal for very strong ones. A general rule for the reader to keep in mind is that a hydrogen bond is roughly ten times weaker than a covalent bond. When two suitable molecules, or two parts of the same molecule, come together, they will readily become connected by a hydrogen bond; but the connection can easily be broken.

An interesting property of a hydrogen bond is its length. This almost always means its length overall—from the center of atom

X to the center of atom Y—since we do not often know the exact
position of the hydrogen atom. In the bifluoride ion, in which
X = Y = F, the overall length is 2.26 Å, which is exceptionally
short. The bonds that concern us are those between an oxygen
atom and nitrogen or another oxygen. With X = Y = O, the
O . . . O distances in recognized hydrogen bonds range from 3.0
to about 2.4 Å. We have mentioned the 2.76 Å in ice. Many carboxylic acids tend to form double molecules; they "dimerize"
through a pair of hydrogen bonds:

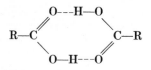

Often the crystalline form of the acid is built from dimers of this
sort, and their dimensions can be measured with x-rays. An example is benzoic acid, C_6H_5COOH, in whose double molecule the
two hydrogen bonds are identical with O . . . O = 2.64 Å. In the
crystal of sodium hydrogen diacetate, $NaH(C_2H_3O_2)_2$, the hydrogen bond between two acetate groups has O . . . O = 2.43 Å.
These three results are typical of weak, moderate, and relatively
strong hydrogen bonds between oxygen atoms.

Hydrogen bonds between an oxygen and a nitrogen atom are
usually longer and weaker than those between oxygens. The sum
of the van der Waals radii is 2.9 Å, so that pairs of atoms separated by much less than this must certainly be engaged in some
sort of bonding. As before, the upper limit for hydrogen bonding
must be increased beyond this to allow for the presence of a
hydrogen atom. In fact N . . . O distances involving recognized
hydrogen bonds range from 3.2 down to about 2.7 Å. Both of the
two possibilities, N—H---O and O—H---N, occur; the former is
probably the one that occurs in some important biological systems to be mentioned later. N—H---N bonds also occur.

We now inquire more closely into the position of the hydrogen
atom—or rather of the proton—within the bond. The commonest
method of inferring the presence of a hydrogen bond is x-ray
diffraction, which tells us that two atoms, X and Y, are a suitable
distance apart. It does not normally locate the hydrogen, though
we know, from the chemical formula of the compound, that one
must be around somewhere. However, we can sometimes get

direct evidence of the hydrogen. A highly accurate x-ray study may provide it; neutron diffraction is better; and spectroscopic work often gives indirect evidence of position. The proton is almost always found to be much nearer to one of the atoms X or Y than to the other. The situation is usually one that can be definitively represented, one way or the other, as O—H---O. The hydroxyl group in this case is recognizable spectroscopically, though its properties are a little changed from those of an isolated group not involved in hydrogen bonding. The proton is not centrally sited.

This may not be true for a very short bond. We know that as the overall O...O length diminishes, the O—H distance tends to increase: the closer the second oxygen atom comes, the more it perturbs the hydroxyl group. So, if the overall length becomes short enough, we should have a genuinely symmetrical bond: O—H—O rather than O—H---O. We do not yet know how short the bond needs to be for this situation to occur or whether it ever occurs between oxygen atoms, but it may obtain in bonds with O...O ≈ 2.4 Å. In the uniquely strong bond in the HF_2^- ion, the bond is almost certainly symmetrical.

Though not normally sited centrally, the proton is usually on the line between X and Y, or very near it. A hydrogen bond is unlikely to be set up unless the arrangement of the molecules is such that this condition can be fulfilled. As sketched in Fig. 5.3a, the angle of the bonds at an oxygen atom is normally within, say,

figure 5.3

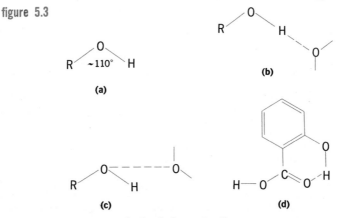

(a)

(b)

(c)

(d)

Conditions affecting hydrogen bonding.

5° either way of 110°; to alter this angle by more than a degree or two requires the input of more energy than the hydrogen bond is worth. Therefore, a bond would be formed if the relative positions of the two molecules were such as to make the R—O---O angle also about 110°, as in Fig. 5.3b, but not if they were those shown in Fig. 5.3c, where the R—O---O angle is about 150°.

An exception occurs to this rule when the hydrogen bond lies within a single molecule, where it is intramolecular, and when the geometry of the molecule forbids the attainment of the best angular arrangement. Salicylic acid, $C_6H_4(OH)COOH$, and its derivatives furnish an example. There is evidence for an intramolecular bond as shown in Fig. 5.3d. Yet the proton lies well off the line of centers between the oxygen atoms. To pull it onto this line, the C—O—H angle would have to be severely distorted to about 90°. As things are, the bond will be a weak one. But the hydrogen atom has to be in some place; and if the O—H group turns so as to put it as close to the carboxylic oxygen atom as possible, there is a small gain in stability, even though it is off the O---O line.

Finally, we may speculate on the nature of hydrogen bonding. How can we explain the attractive force giving rise to a bond with the properties described above? Two types of explanation have been given. The first is that the force is essentially electrostatic, resembling the dipole-dipole attraction described on page 95. When two atoms X and Y form a hydrogen bond, both elements must be highly electronegative. This implies that both X—H and Y—M (where M stands for the remainder of the molecule to which Y belongs) will carry dipole moments in the senses indicated by the partial charges

$$\overset{\delta-}{X}—\overset{\delta+}{H} \qquad \overset{\delta-}{Y}—\overset{\delta+}{M}$$

(In some cases Y may be an anion, with a full negative charge, as in the bifluoride ion: $\overset{\delta-}{F}—\overset{\delta+}{H}---\overset{-}{F}$.) Either way, there will be an attractive force between the units: H and Y, which bear opposite charges, are closer together than are X and Y, which bear like charges, so that the electrostatic attraction between the first pair exceeds the repulsion between the second. The net attraction is greater than it would be in an ordinary dipole-dipole interaction because the small size of the hydrogen atom allows X—H and Y—M to come closer together than two ordinary dipolar molecules could.

The second explanation involves a wave-mechanical effect, and it can be put most simply in VB or resonance terms. Though we have not hitherto shown it explicitly, atom Y always carries a lone pair of electrons, and its high electronegativity guarantees that this pair is effective. We can therefore write alternative bond diagrams as follows:

$$X—H \quad :Y—M \quad \text{and} \quad X: H\text{———}Y—M$$
$$(a) \qquad\qquad\qquad\qquad (b)$$

According to VB theory, there will be resonance between these two forms; the true structure is intermediate between (a) and (b) and therefore has lower energy and is more stable.

However, for the situation we have actually shown above, the stabilization will be slight. As is normally found, we have put the proton much nearer to X than to Y. Form (b) thus has an unnaturally long covalent bond between H and Y, since resonating forms must have their atomic nuclei in the same positions, or nearly so. The bond will therefore be strained and have an inherently higher energy than (a). Stated informally, there will be little resonance; the participation of form (b) will be insignificant, and the resonance energy will be inadequate to account for the observed strengths of hydrogen bonds.

The outcome is that hydrogen bonding is mainly due to the electrostatic effect. In the majority of cases, any additional resonance stabilization is of only secondary importance.

We have seen that in unusually short hydrogen bonds the proton is nearer to the midpoint and that, if the bond is short enough, it might possibly become symmetrical. In these circumstances, the objection to the resonance explanation disappears; the two forms (a) and (b) become equivalent, and (b) does not now have the unnaturally long covalent bond. So we may qualify the statement of the preceding paragraph by adding that any resonance contribution to the total binding energy will increase as the bond becomes shorter and that it may become important in very short hydrogen bonds.

We cannot better illustrate the significance of hydrogen bonding in biological systems than by its role in the structures of proteins and nucleic acids.

Protein molecules consist of a large number of amino acid units strung together. Amino acids are represented by the general formula $RCH(NH_2)CO_2H$, in which variation of the nature of the group R gives rise to a score or more of different compounds. As we saw on page 75, amino acid molecules can link themselves together, by loss of the elements of water with the formation of peptide linkage, in the following manner:

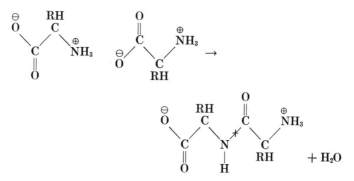

The peptide linkage is the bond marked with a cross. Study of the molecular dimensions of a number of simple polypeptides shows that this N—C bond is always much shorter than would be expected for a single bond between carbon and nitrogen—about 1.32 Å rather than 1.47 Å. The interpretation is that the bond possesses double-bond character, which prevents free rotation about it. The situation resembles that in an ethylenic derivative and has the consequence that the six atoms—the nitrogen and carbon with the four other atoms directly bonded to them—must be coplanar or nearly so. On the other hand, the N—C and C—C bonds adjacent to the peptide link have substantially normal single-bond lengths, and about them twisting of the molecular chain occurs readily.

The great variety of proteins comes about because there are twenty different amino acids which may be arranged in any order in chains of (usually) more than a hundred units. Changing the nature of one unit at any point in the chain will give a protein with different properties. The number of possibilities is enormous—

indeed, theoretically infinite if we place no upper limit on the chain length.

By chemical and biochemical methods we can determine the sequence of the amino acids in a given protein. Though this is a difficult task, it has already been fully worked out in a number of important cases. But even when this has been done, we are still a long way from understanding the structure of the protein molecule. A long-chain molecule can adopt a multitude of shapes, or conformations, by internal twisting about the bonds along the chain (pages 66 and 72). Linus Pauling, R. B. Corey, and H. R. Branson, in 1951, however, suggested a particular form of twisting, which, though it certainly does not occur in all types of proteins, has been very useful in furthering our understanding of proteins generally and which has proved to be correct in the only types of protein of which we now have any detailed structural information. These are myoglobin and hemoglobin.*

In developing their theory, Pauling, Corey, and Branson produced a striking example of scientific method. They started from the reliable information then available on the molecules of simple peptides, which contain two or three amino acid units. They assumed that the structural principles there revealed would apply to the much longer polypeptide chains in actual proteins. Hence they were able to make confident predictions, which have now been confirmed.

Among the assumptions made by Pauling, Corey, and Branson three are particularly relevant here: (1) that the six atoms about the peptide linkage would be coplanar, (2) that bond lengths and bond angles throughout the chain would have values similar to those established in simple molecules, and (3) that the chain might form itself into a spiral, or helix, by internal twisting about the nonpeptide bonds, so as to allow all the NH and CO groups to form hydrogen bonds with N ... O distances not very different from 2.79 Å. On investigating all possibilities, they found that there were only two which exactly satisfied all their conditions. These are known as the α and β helices. Low and Baybutt shortly afterward found a third, π, helix which would also satisfy the conditions laid down within a tolerance that would probably be

---

* The α helix has also been found recently (1965) in the molecule of lysozyme.

acceptable. All three were theoretical possibilities. It is the α helix that has been found experimentally in the molecules of myoglobin and hemoglobin.

We can simplify our explanation of the problem by omitting the hydrogen atom and the side group R from one of the carbon atoms and by starting with the other atoms of the chain in an extended flat zigzag. The resulting conformation, obtainable by appropriate twistings about the nonpeptide bonds, is sketched in Fig. 5.4a.

The peptide links are marked as before. We note that the C=O and N—H groups each point alternately up and down. Now, by twisting the molecule about C—C and the nonpeptide C—N bonds (which can be done without impairing the coplanarity of the atoms around the peptide link), the molecule can be put into a form in which all the N—H bonds point upward and all the C=O downward. This is schematically represented in Fig. 5.4b, though the molecule is now no longer flat. Instead, it has taken on a helical shape such as that illustrated in Fig. 5.5. In this conformation the C=O group of one amino acid unit comes into such a juxtaposition with the N—H of the third unit away that

figure 5.4

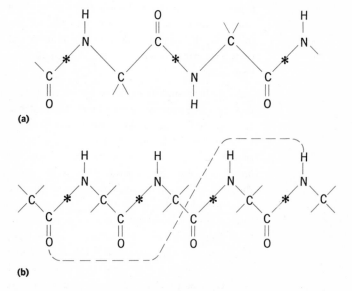

(a)

(b)

Peptide chain: (a) extended, planar conformation and (b) schematic representation of the nonplanar form which leads to the helix. The peptide linkages are marked with asterisks, and the broken line indicates the hydrogen bonding between successive turns of the helix.

figure 5.5

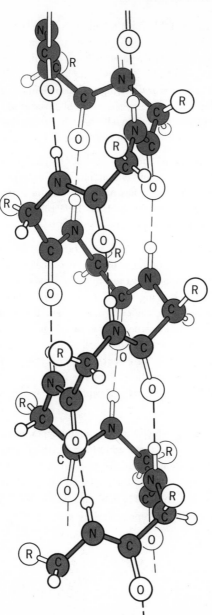

The right-handed α helix found in some protein molecules and predicted by Pauling, Corey, and Branson. (From an amended diagram very kindly supplied by Prof. R. B. Corey.)

they can comfortably form a hydrogen bond of the correct length. One such hydrogen bond is indicated by the broken line of Fig. 5.4b, where it can easily be seen that it completes a ring of thirteen atoms (O, C, N, C, C, N, C, C, N, C, C, N, H). Figure 5.5 shows this bond in its natural setting and also shows that all the groups are enabled to form these bonds, which serve to "fix" the helix. The energy evolved when all these hydrogen bonds are formed stabilizes this particular conformation of the molecule.

A special feature of the helix is that the pitch of the spiral is not simple. There are about 3.6 amino acid units per turn. In other words, when the chain has made one complete turn, the units do not lie exactly over one another. Five turns are needed to yield an almost exact superposition.

In 1953 Francis H. C. Crick and James D. Watson suggested a general structure for the molecule of a nucleic acid. The conception and development of their hypothesis bear a close resemblance to those of the Pauling-Corey theory of the helices. Here, too, we have a biological molecule of great size and formidable complexity. An hypothesis of its structure was based on a careful consideration of the known dimensions of much simpler molecules, and hydrogen bonding played an essential part in the proposed structure. The hypothesis has been supported by nearly all subsequent work and is now generally accepted as a major advance in biological science.

Nucleic acids, of which there are many types, occur in the nucleus of the cell and are the medium by which genetic information is passed on from mother to daughter when the cell divides. As was the case with proteins, their general chemical nature had been known for some time. The molecule contains a long chain, a section of which can be represented by Fig. 5.6. S signifies a molecule

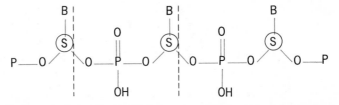

Linking of nucleotide units in a nucleic acid chain. S represents the sugar residue and B the base.

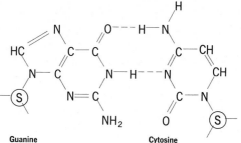

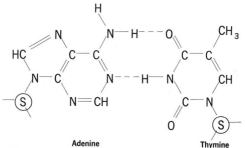

The four types of base molecule and the permissible ways in which they may be paired by hydrogen bonding. S represents the sugar residues by which the units are joined to phosphoric acid residues and thus linked into the two complementary chains.

of a sugar-type substance, normally deoxyribose; to this is attached a molecule* of an organic base *B*. This base is, almost always, one of four possibilities: guanine, *G*; cytosine, *C*; adenine, *A*; or thymine, *T*, whose formulas are given in Fig. 5.7. *G* and *A* belong to the type of bases known as purines; *C* and *T* are pyrimidines. The compound unit consisting of deoxyribose and a base is known as a *nucleoside*.

The nucleosides are strung together, to give the long chain, by phosphoric acid groups, as indicated in Fig. 5.6. The actual repeat unit is marked by the broken lines; comprising the phosphoric acid and the nucleoside units, it is known as a *nucleotide*. In the molecule of a typical nucleic acid, such as deoxyribonucleic acid (DNA), there are chains of this kind incorporating many thousands of nucleotide units.

---

* The word "molecule" is not quite accurate here, since the elements of water are lost when two of them unite. "Residue" is a more correct word.

On the basis of this general information, together with our knowledge of the dimensions and stereochemistry of simpler molecules and of the properties of nucleic acids (particularly toward x-rays), Crick and Watson developed the following theory.

The molecule consists of two long nucleotide chains of the sort just described. Each chain is twisted into a spiral form. The spirals intertwine in a manner, sketched in Fig. 5.8, which allows the chains to maintain parallelism with each other. They are held thus by pairs of hydrogen bonds between the base residues of each chain. This sets up a sequence of internal "struts" between the two chains. A detailed consideration of scale models convinced Crick and Watson that this hydrogen bonding between the chains would occur only if a purine of one chain linked itself with a pyrimidine of the other. Moreover, the linking must be even more specific: a good fit could be achieved only with guanine linked to cytosine or adenine to thymine. Hydrogen bonding between appropriate pairs of bases is indicated in Fig. 5.7. With this pairing, but not with any other, the length of the strut is kept constant. If adenine were linked with guanine, for instance, the strut would be much too long.

We cannot do justice to this ingenious theory here. We emphasize merely the part played by hydrogen bonding and the consequent *complementarity* of the two chains. Because of the stringent condition governing base-pairing, it follows that, if the two chains of a single molecule are split apart and if each single chain is then able to regenerate the molecule by selecting from its environment the necessary nucleotide units to construct another chain for itself, then the new chains must have exactly the same sequence of bases as the originals. For instance, suppose one chain of the original molecule had a section running $...A—C—T—A—G...$; its partner must have matched this with $...T—G—A—T—C...$, since guanine must link with cytosine and adenine with thymine. When the chains become separated, each may regenerate a complementary chain: the $...A—C—T—A—G...$ section forms for itself a $...T—G—A—T—C...$ section, while $...T—G—A—T—C...$ forms $...A—C—T—A—G...$. Genetic information can therefore be coded by a particular sequence of thousands of nucleotide units, and this information can be handed on to the next generation by a replication process.

figure 5.8

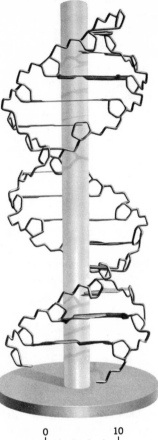

Crick-Watson theory of the structure of nucleic acid molecules. [By courtesy of Dr. Crick, based on a diagram in *Proc. Roy. Soc. (London)*, 223A: Fig. 5 (1954).]

organizational forces between molecules

We may now usefully summarize our concept of the molecule in its environment. Primarily, molecules are groups of atoms held together by covalent bonds. These bonds are strong and hold the atoms in position fairly rigidly. To be more precise, there is an order of precedence in the rigidity with which a molecule opposes different kinds of distortion. As was described on page 67, bond stretching, bond bending, and bond twisting are in order of increasing ease of distortion. In the first two ways the shape of a molecule cannot be altered very significantly.

Twisting about a double bond is also difficult; about a single bond it is much easier. Rotation of the parts of a molecule about a single bond is not quite free, though the phrase "free rotation" is often applied. But there are often three most favorable conformations about a bond, and but little energy is required to twist the molecule from one conformation to another. By a series of conformational changes at some of its single bonds, the overall shape of a large molecule can be drastically altered, and this can be done with expenditure of little energy.

A force which controls the shape of a molecule by influencing these conformations is known as an *organizational force*. The hydrogen bonding in proteins is a notable example. The *primary structure* of a protein molecule consists of the chain of amino acid residues linked by the peptide bond, which is also covalent, with special properties owing to its possession of some double-bond character. When this chain takes on a particular series of conformations at each single bond, the resulting helix is well adapted for stabilization by hydrogen bonding between each NH group and a CO group in the next turn of the spiral. These hydrogen bonds can thus be said to organize the molecule; they give it a *secondary structure*.

In the single protein of which we have at present direct and detailed structural knowledge (myoglobin) this secondary helical structure has been observed. A helix can be either right- or left-handed, and either form of the α helix is theoretically possible. In fact, the helix in myoglobin, and no doubt in hemoglobin, too, turns out to have the right-handed pitch shown in Fig. 5.5. This means that, if we imagine ourselves to be walking along the inside of the spiral, the polypeptide chain would appear to turn in a clockwise direction, as would the thread of an ordinary screw. (This is true whichever way we walk along the helix.)

Considerable straight stretches of the chain are in this helical form. But at intervals the direction of the helix changes abruptly, thus giving the protein a *tertiary structure*. At these bends the regularity of the secondary structure breaks down temporarily. The factors which organize the tertiary structure are not yet properly understood. What is certain is that the biologic functioning of a globular protein depends critically on the particular way in which the helical chains are thus folded. When the tertiary structure is changed, the properties of the protein change drastically.

The succession of amino acids in the chain of a particular protein constitutes the primary structure and gives rise to the secondary structure; the general tendency to form as many hydrogen bonds as possible gives a helical shape to the chain. But at certain specific points this tendency is overruled. This allows the helix to be interrupted and to change direction, thus constituting a tertiary structure. The presumption is that all this is inherent in the original amino acid sequence.

author's note At one point in this chapter a molecule is described as "clever," and throughout the book there are similar phrases which might seem to endow the molecules with sapience, or at least with a nose for profit so far as energy is concerned. This impression might be enhanced if the thesis of the next chapter were to be slightly misunderstood. Perhaps the author should therefore disclaim any intention of advancing an anthropomorphic view of molecules, which—he believes—inevitably behave as they do because of the properties of the fundamental particles of which they are composed.

All the same, an affectation of familiarity with the habits of molecules will do little harm to the reader so long as he always recognizes its essential artificiality. An intuitive feeling about molecules, as concrete realities, is a useful faculty for the student of chemistry or of biochemistry to develop. The student need not be discouraged from following Professor Wald's advice and asking himself, "How would I behave if I were that molecule?"

6

the fitness of the environment

the organism and its environment

This chapter copies the title of a book by L. J. Henderson (1878–1942), of Harvard, which was published in 1913. A classic of biological science, its theme is illustrated in the following quotations:

> The fitness of the environment is one part of a reciprocal relationship of which the fitness of the organism is the other. . . . (The fitness) is not less frequently evident in the characteristics of water, carbonic acid, and the compounds of carbon, hydrogen and oxygen than is fitness from adaptation in the characteristics of the organism.

> Given matter, energy, and the resulting necessity that life shall be a mechanism, the conclusion follows that the atmosphere of solid bodies does actually provide the best of all possible environments for life.*

We shall try to expound this theme in simple terms. Consideration of organic evolution has familiarized us with the notion that living organisms have adapted themselves to their environment and that they have done this, in general, by becoming increasingly complex, with more and more specialized parts. They have become increasingly fitted to use their environment and to control it: from the bacterium floating in the primeval ocean to Homo sapiens in an air-conditioned room.

Part of the converse is also familiar. Organisms have reacted on their environment so as to change it, and thus it has become fitted for more efficient organisms. On a small scale this is illustrated by the various species of microbes which take their turns during the fermentation of a compost heap. On a much vaster scale are the interactions between living creatures and the earth's

---

* From the context it appears that the rather strange phrase "atmosphere of solid bodies" means the matter actually present in the universe, taken together with its properties.

atmosphere. Initially the atmosphere must have contained much carbon dioxide and little free oxygen; evolving life has reversed this composition, so that much more efficient oxidative reactions can be used by the more complex forms of life.

But Henderson's concept of fitness goes much deeper than this. The environment seems to be well fitted for the sustenance of life in ways over which the organism has no control and which, indeed, predate the existence of the organism. Much of his book is taken up with a detailed description of this environmental fitness and we shall recapitulate it later in the chapter. Of course, some aspects of this fitness had been recognized at least a century before Henderson's time, and they had been used as evidence for creative design. Henderson is careful to avoid such teleological arguments, not because they are necessarily untrue, but because arguments from design have always been fruitless in science. He quotes Bacon to the effect that final causes are like vestal virgins: "They are dedicated to God, and are barren."

Nevertheless, the respects in which the environment seems uniquely fitted for the development of life are numerous and very striking. They can hardly be dismissed as coincidences. If we are to reject teleological hypotheses, then at least we must suspect the operation of some deep natural law of which we are at present ignorant. Henderson considers it to be some compensation for our ignorance that we may here have a proof

...that... peculiar and unsuspected relationships exist between the properties of matter and the phenomena of life; that the process of cosmic evolution is indissolubly linked with the fundamental characteristics of the organism; that logically, in some obscure manner, cosmic and biological evolution are one.

First we wish to restate the evidence for the proposition that the properties of matter are particularly well adapted for the development and evolution of life. In doing this, we shall merely be summarizing what was done—and done far better—by Henderson more than a half century ago. Where we have some advantage over him now is in our fuller understanding of atomic and molecular structure. We are therefore in a position to put the fitness of the environment a stage deeper into the nature of matter. That is what we propose to do in the remainder of the chapter.

the basic physical and chemical requirements

To define what we mean by life is technically and logically difficult, and a rough, working description must serve our immediate needs. Life is revealed by chemical changes which occur in certain types of molecules. These molecules are extremely large and complex. They are composed mainly of the elements carbon, hydrogen, and oxygen; but a number of other elements are essential in smaller proportions, notably nitrogen, phosphorus, sulfur, and iron or magnesium, and some others in traces. Certain elements are needed in ionic form, notably sodium, potassium, calcium, magnesium, and chlorine.

The large biological molecules can take part in chemical reactions with much simpler molecules. These reactions have two aspects: first, they can lead to the utilization of energy, which is essential for the activities of life; second, they enable complex molecules to construct, from simple units, other complex molecules sometimes identical with themselves, sometimes not. The energy comes ultimately from sunlight, though only plants can utilize solar energy directly. The simple molecular units are notably oxygen, carbon dioxide, and water, though some others must obviously be necessary as sources of nitrogen and the other essential elements.

The molecules that characteristically constitute living organisms must be large and complex. This is basically because they have to carry a vast amount of "information." We see this in an extreme form with DNA (page 115), one molecule—or perhaps a few molecules—of which carries all the genetic information necessary for reproducing another representative of the organism. A single fertilized cell might, for example, develop into a particular species of bird not only with the correct physical characteristics but also with the capability of flight and adopting innumerable other types of instinctive behavior when necessary. The same kind of feature can be seen in a protein molecule, which has its highly specific function to fulfill. The number, type, and sequence of the amino acid residues in the polypeptide chain are decisive of the exact way in which the chain arranges itself, and hence of the biological properties of the protein. Many millions—probably many billions—of different kinds of proteins are capable of existing. So with proteins, as with DNA, the problem is one of coding: the numbers and the sequence of simple units must carry information of a very detailed sort. At least some biological molecules must therefore be large and complex. A small molecule just could not carry the load.

The large molecules must have other qualities besides complexity. They must be reasonably easy to build up according to specification, and once built, they must be reasonably stable. At the same time, they must not be too stable, because being alive implies the occurrence of chemical reactions when necessary. Minerals may have fairly complex structure, but they are too stable; they cannot be changed without exposure to very high temperatures or to chemical reagents acting for a very long period of time.

The element carbon is uniquely suited for the construction of large, complex molecules. The known compounds of carbon are much more numerous than are those of all the other elements put together. This is primarily because a carbon atom can form stable covalent bonds with other carbon atoms, and the process can continue almost without limit.

The prototype of any organic molecule is a hydrocarbon. This consists of a number of carbon atoms linked into a chain which may or may not be branched and which may contain double bonds or be closed into one or more rings. Since the covalence of carbon is almost invariably 4, the bonds not required by other carbon atoms are used to hold hydrogen atoms.

Now comes the possibility of replacing some of these hydrogens by atoms of other elements (substitution). In particular, oxygen and nitrogen, which come directly after carbon in the periodic table, can substitute for hydrogen very readily. Not only does this ring the changes on the original hydrocarbon, it also makes the substituted molecule polar and gives it acidic or basic properties, notably by the carboxyl ($-COOH$) and amino ($-NH_2$) groups, respectively. Furthermore, such polar groups enable molecules to link themselves together to form larger ones. We have seen examples of this in the peptide link (page 74) and in the hydrogen bonding in proteins and in DNA (page 110). It also occurs in the buildup of starch and cellulose from simple sugar molecules.

Fluorine also forms strong bonds with carbon, but this is not of biological value. Partly this is because the C—F bond is too strong. Fluorocarbons have technological uses just because they are so much more stable than hydrocarbons. But the chief reason why fluorine is biologically unimportant is that it is univalent. It therefore cannot link other units together, as can oxygen or nitrogen.

Other atoms besides carbon have the capacity of forming covalent bonds with atoms of their own kind. Silicon and sulfur do it readily. However, the molecules thus formed are much less stable. This leads us to recognize another peculiarity of carbon: its valence cannot exceed 4, since atoms of elements in the first short period cannot exceed the octet of electrons. There are only four orbitals for its valence electrons: the single $2s$ and the three $2p$. There is no $2d$ orbital, while the orbitals of the third shell ($3s$, $3p$, and $3d$) require any electrons they may accommodate to have too high an energy for useful bonding. Carbon forms four strong covalent bonds and only four, so that the carbon skeleton of a molecule is rather stable. By contrast, similar compounds of silicon, for example, are very unstable. Silicon has a larger atom than carbon, and it can make use of $3d$ orbitals to raise its valence to 6. A molecule with a skeleton of quadrivalent silicon atoms would therefore be susceptible to attack and decomposition by chemical reagents.

Biological molecules must not be too stable. As we have already stated, life implies the possibility of appropriate chemical changes. Reactivity in carbon compounds is provided by two means: substitution of one or more hydrogen atoms by oxygen or nitrogen and the presence of double bonds. True double bonds are found only with small atoms, and they are largely restricted to carbon, nitrogen, and oxygen. Wald has stressed the fact that the elements hydrogen, oxygen, nitrogen, and carbon have the smallest atoms that can satisfy themselves by accepting (respectively) one, two, three, and four electrons.

The stability—or, on the other hand, the reactivity—of a molecule cannot be properly discussed without regard to the temperature. The principles here are two: that all chemical reactions are greatly accelerated by rise of temperature; and that—partly, though not wholly—for this reason large and complex molecules cannot exist at high temperatures. In the form in which we know it, life can function only in a narrow range of temperature, between, say, 0 and 50°C. If the temperature should fall much below 0°, the chemical reactions which constitute life in its mechanistic sense would become impossibly slow. Most living things would die; at best, only some of the simplest organisms might survive in a state of dormancy. If the temperature should rise too high, the necessary chemical reactions would become too rapid.

To be sure, many of the more highly evolved creatures have some form of thermostating device, but such devices can cope with only a moderate degree of hotness in the environment. Undue acceleration of proper reactions is not the only trouble. A protein molecule becomes inherently unstable at a slightly elevated temperature. The tertiary structure is soon lost; then hydrogen bonds break, with destruction of the secondary structure; and finally general chemical decomposition ensues, with fission of the peptide links. Nucleic acids would suffer a similar fate.

The temperature range within which life, as we know it, is conceivable corresponds roughly with that within which water is a liquid. This is one of Henderson's instances of the fitness of the environment, and if it is a coincidence, it is a remarkable one. We shall discuss the peculiar properties of water in relation to life later.

We now know a good deal about the elements and their chemical properties. These properties are presumably the same in every part of the universe, and it seems impossible that any other light elements can exist besides those known to us on earth. Given that life must be based on chemical transactions, we can conclude that it must involve large molecules; that such large molecules, combining adequate stability with adequate variability and reactivity, can occur only among compounds with a skeleton of carbon atoms carrying hydrogen and a few other types of substituent atoms; and that these molecules can function only within a temperature range in which water is liquid. Experience shows that it is unwise to declare that something is scientifically impossible, but it is hard to imagine any other *chemical* basis for life.

We may recapitulate the main argument of this section: Carbon is almost always quadrivalent: it forms four strong bonds and only four. When these valences are linked to other carbon atoms and to hydrogen, stable molecules result, and there is virtually no limit to their size and complexity. Points of reactivity and variations can be introduced into such molecules by the occurrence of double bonds or by the substitution of certain other atoms or groups for hydrogen; these groups are —OH, =O, —NH₂, and =NH in particular. Interactions between such substituent groups give rise to further possibilities of size and complexity in the construction of large molecules. Such complex molecules can be stable, and at the same time sufficiently reactive, only if the temperature lies within the liquidity range of water.

the role of other elements in biological chemistry

Living matter is mainly composed of the elements H, C, N, and O, and we have outlined some of the reasons for this. A number of other elements are also essential, though only in smaller proportions and sometimes merely as traces. We may consider what roles some of these are called upon to play.

Some elements occur simply as ions. Na^+, K^+, and Cl^- are important in the physical chemistry of biological processes, but they do not enter into the structures of biological molecules. The calcium ion, Ca^{++}, is required for the construction of bone, which is essential in the structural engineering of many animals. Bone can, very roughly, be regarded as a calcium phosphate "mineral," which is precipitated when sufficient concentrations of calcium and phosphate ions occur together in solution:

$$Ca^{++} + \text{phosphate ion} \rightarrow \text{bone}$$

A formal *solubility product* can be stated, so that the reaction proceeds from left to right when the product of the concentrations of the two sorts of ions exceeds a critical value. But the matter is nothing like so simple as this schematic equation would suggest. Bone contains many other materials besides calcium phosphate.

Some transitional elements are essential, and they may function for two reasons. First, such elements can exist at different oxidation levels. For instance, iron occurs as the ferrous ion, Fe^{++}, with 24 electrons, and as the ferric ion, Fe^{3+}, with 23. The reaction

$$Fe^{3+} + e^- \rightleftharpoons Fe^{++}$$

represents a simple oxidation-reduction change; on addition of the electron e^-, the ferric ion becomes reduced to ferrous, and vice versa. Such changes may be linked—probably in an indirect way—with oxidation-reduction processes among biological molecules. Second, the transitional elements form coordination complexes (see page 40). A large organic molecule may be chelated to the metallic ion by way of, say, four nitrogen atoms.

The oxidation-reduction reaction occurs while the transitional metal is involved in a complex of this sort. Thus the two functions are closely connected. Hemoglobin is a familiar example: the operative part of the molecule is the heme group, a coordination complex of iron whose function is the picking up and transport of an oxygen molecule (see page 90). Magnesium, though not a transitional element and not existing in two oxidation levels, occupies a similar site in the molecule of chlorophyll.

There are two other elements which seem to be essential for all forms of life. These are sulfur and, particularly, phosphorus. Sulfur occurs in the amino acid methionine and the related amino acids cystine and cysteine, and it is therefore a constituent of proteins. Phosphorus occurs as derivatives of phosphoric acid, H_3PO_4, which may be represented by formula (1). One or two of the hydrogen atoms may be replaced by organic radicals (R_1 and R_2), as indicated by (2), to yield *phosphate esters*. The resulting

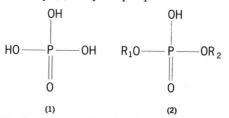

(1)   (2)

molecule will still be an acid, since it retains one or two of its hydroxylic hydrogen atoms. The various nucleosides are strung together in this way in the molecules of the nucleic acids. In this form phosphorus plays an important part in the genetic system. The participation of ATP (adenosine triphosphate) in·muscle contraction reminds us that phosphate esters are involved in many biological reactions.

We may ask why it should be phosphoric acid, rather than some other acid, whose esters play this important part. We may suggest an answer by recapitulating the considerations given on page 54. The molecule of phosphoric acid or of its esters can be represented as having only an octet of electrons around the phosphorus atom, as indicated by formula (3). But the $3d$ orbitals of the phosphorus atom are also available, and we believe that at least one of them can be used to accommodate a pair of electrons from one of the oxygen atoms, as was implied in formulas (1) and (2) and as is shown in (4). We may put this a little more

(3)   (4)

precisely in VB terminology by stating that any of the P—O bonds may have some double-bond character because the molecule is a resonance hybrid between (3) and such forms as (4). In different phosphate esters the participation of (3) and (4) may differ, with a consequent difference in the amount of double-bond character and in the bond strength. Therefore, different phosphate esters may liberate widely different amounts of energy when they are decomposed. This possibility is one way to provide a flexibility in the energetics of biological reactions.

water Life on earth requires water, and it is hard to conceive of any form of vital activity in the absence of water. Life is supposed to have originated in the sea, which not only provided a medium in which the primitive organism could float around but also carried in solution the basic chemical materials required to maintain life. A liquid would be essential. A solid medium would not allow rapid enough movement of dissolved substances, while a gas would be too light to carry any except other gaseous materials. When evolving life moved out of the sea into fresh water, or onto the dry land, it could do so only because organisms were able to take something of their marine environment with them. The blood and other body fluids can be regarded as deriving from the primeval ocean.

No other liquid is so suitable as is water for the support of life, and its unusual and surprising properties all seem to be deviations from normality in a sense favorable for this purpose. The uniqueness of water has been realized for at least 150 years, and the theme was developed in great detail by Henderson, who classified the peculiarities of water under twelve headings. We shall restrict ourselves to a few of these peculiarities that are of the most obvious importance.

table 6.1 **the melting and boiling points of some hydrides, °C**

	OH$_2$	SH$_2$	SeH$_2$	TeH$_2$
m.p.	0	−86	−64	−57
b.p.	100	−61	−42	−2
Range	100	25	22	55

	CH$_4$	NH$_3$	OH$_2$	FH
m.p.	−186	−78	0	−83
b.p.	−161	−33	100	19
Range	25	45	100	102

The first remarkable thing about water is that it is a liquid at all. Table 6.1 compares the boiling points of water and some closely related compounds. The upper part of the table gives the temperatures for the hydrides of the group VI elements. Descending the group from tellurium to sulfur, the boiling point decreases with decreasing molecular weight, so that a rough extrapolation would suggest a temperature of about −80°C for the boiling point of oxygen hydride (OH$_2$). In fact, the boiling point is 180° higher than our guess. Now consider the lower part of the table. The molecular weights of methane, ammonia, water, and hydrogen fluoride are all about the same; yet water has by far the highest boiling point. It is the only compound in the table to be a liquid at ordinary temperatures. The melting points, which are also given, show a similar tendency; ice has by far the highest value. That water retains liquidity over a long range of temperature and that this includes the range within which proteins are stable, yet appropriately reactive, are facts of the greatest importance for living organisms.

Water has a very high specific heat, much higher than any other simple liquid except ammonia. A lot of heat needs to be added or withdrawn to raise or lower its temperature, so that a mass of water tends to maintain its temperature. Water is more "self-thermostating" than other substances. For instance, the temperature of the ocean varies much less than does that of the continental land mass. This is a valuable property from the biological point of view, since metabolic processes occur at convenient rates only within a narrow temperature range.

Water has the almost unique property that it solidifies to a material which is less dense than the liquid, and—even more unusual—between 4 and 0°C the density of the liquid decreases with fall of temperature. The importance of these properties for life is immense. In cold weather the surface of the sea or of a large lake freezes, leaving the liquid below at a substantially uniform temperature. If water were free from these anomalies, the coldest water would sink to the bottom, and there it would freeze. Re-melting, when the weather became warmer, would be a slow and difficult process. Polar and subpolar waters would consist mainly of ice all the year round, and life could hardly have developed in surface pools which would freeze up again each winter.

Water has a higher latent heat of evaporation than has any other liquid; it requires a larger input of heat before it can evaporate. This has advantageous consequences. For one, the evaporation of sweat is an effective method for maintaining a constant body temperature in hot climates. This is an essential mechanism among higher animals. But the property favors life at all levels indirectly. Surface water evaporates relatively slowly. Life in most forms would be impossible if every lake or pond and most rivers dried up during the summer.

The high latent heat of evaporation has a subtler, secondary consequence that favors life. By a thermodynamic law, a high latent heat requires a high *rate of change* of vapor pressure with temperature. The vapor pressure of water is low at low tempera-tures but, as the temperature rises, increases more rapidly than do the vapor pressures of normal liquids. For example, it rises from 9 mm at 10°C to 55 mm at 40°C, an increase of sixfold, whereas the vapor pressure of benzene rises from 47 to 177 mm, an increase of less than fourfold. This again assists the thermo-static properties of water: the rapidly rising vapor pressure makes for greater cooling efficiency.

In addition to being an essential chemical material for life, water has the equally essential function of acting as a solvent. It carries other substances in solution. Again we find a unique property. Water is the best known solvent for ionic compounds. Salts are insoluble in most liquids, but many of them are water soluble. Water will also dissolve most small organic molecules provided they carry a polar group such as —OH, —NH_2, or —COOH. On the other hand, molecules which consist largely of hydrocarbon (such as those of the fats) do not dissolve in water. The effective solubilization of proteins and other large molecules in certain circumstances involves surface activity. Here another unique property of water helps: its high surface tension gives rise to unusual behavior at its surface. This topic of colloid chemistry is of the greatest biological significance, but it is too complex for us to discuss further.

Oxygen is not very soluble in water, but it is about twice as soluble as nitrogen is. Animal life in water depends on the availability of dissolved oxygen, so that this property is important. At 0°C a given volume of water dissolves about one-twentieth of its volume of oxygen when this gas is at a pressure of one atmosphere.

the behavior of water as a function of its molecular properties

We shall not attempt any fundamental "explanation" of the unique fitness of water for the support of life. But we are in a position to relate its peculiar properties to what we know of the water molecule, and hence to tie these two sets of facts together by giving them a common cause. This is the most that is ordinarily meant by scientific explanation.

We have already discussed the water molecule (pages 37, 45, and 71), but we may summarize its main features. The atomic nuclei are in a bent relationship, with the H—O—H angle about 105°. The O—H distances are each about 0.95 Å. The molecule is polar; the hydrogen atoms carry partial positive charges which are balanced by equal negative charges on the oxygen. Remembering that the van der Waals radius of oxygen is about 1.4 Å (i.e., that most of the electron density is contained within a sphere of this radius), we may regard the water molecule as a roughly spherical object of radius 1.4 Å with partial charges at four points near its periphery. These partial charges are in a tetrahedral relationship, making angles of about 110° with one another at the center; two of the charges are positive, near the hydrogen atoms, and two negative, as suggested in Fig. 6.1a.

In the gaseous state, these molecules exist independently of each other. In the liquid or solid states, the molecules of water (as of all substances) crowd together much more closely. In a rough-and-ready phrase, we may say that they come into contact. It is quite easy to calculate what would be the density of water if its molecules crowded together in an uncomplicated way. A formula of trigonometry tells us that $\dfrac{1}{4\sqrt{2r^3}}$ spheres of radius r can

figure 6.1

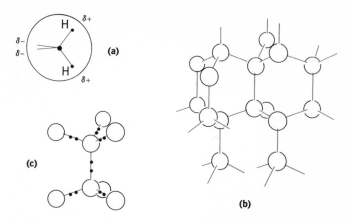

(a) The water molecule, with emphasis on the sites of its partial charges. (b) The structure of ice. Only the oxygen atoms are shown, and the lines between them represent hydrogen bonds. (c) The dis-ordering of the protons in ice. The small, dark circles mark alternative sites for the protons. There can be only one proton between each pair of neighboring oxygen atoms; but there is statistically a 50:50 chance of finding it in one or other of the two possible sites.

be packed into unit volume. This corresponds to the optimal conditions of close packing, in which each sphere is surrounded by 12 immediate neighbors. With each molecule given a radius of 1.4×10^{-8} cm and a mass of 18 g/Avogadro number, we calculate the density as follows:

$$\text{Density} = \frac{18}{6 \times 10^{23} \times 4\sqrt{2} \times (1.4)^3 \times 10^{-24}} = 1.93 \text{ g/cm}^3$$

So the actual density of water is little more than one-half of what it would be if the molecules were closed packed. Ice has a density of 0.92 g/cm^3, which is less than half that calculated.

We get a clue to the anomalous density of water by first considering ice, which, being a crystalline solid, can be conveniently studied by x-ray and other diffraction methods (page 60). X-rays indicate the relative positions of the oxygen atoms. As sketched in Fig. 6.1b, each atom has four nearest neighbors, which lie in tetrahedral directions at a distance of 2.76 Å. The hydrogen atoms are not detected in an ordinary x-ray analysis; but the O . . . O distance implies a hydrogen bond (page 104), so that we may confidently infer that each such contact between a pair of oxygens involves one hydrogen atom. This situation, with every hydrogen linked to two oxygens and every oxygen linked to four hydrogens (and thence on to four other oxygens), adds up correctly to an overall composition $H:O = 2:1$.

Though not directly relevant to our present discussion, the positions actually occupied by the hydrogen atoms is of great interest. We have stated on page 107, that in most hydrogen bonds—and certainly in one as long as 2.76 Å—the proton is closer to one oxygen atom than to the other; that is to say, (1) the proton is strongly (covalently) bonded to one oxygen to form a recognizable hydroxyl group and (2) the hydrogen bond consists essentially of the electrostatic attraction between the OH group and the other oxygen atom. The positions of the protons in ice can be studied by the diffraction of electrons, and more particularly of neutrons. What is found is that there are—apparently—two *half*-hydrogens along each O...O line in positions about 1.00 Å, and 1.76 Å, from each oxygen atom (see Fig. 6.1c). This appearance cannot be literally true; we cannot have genuine "half atoms." What it means is that there is a 50:50 chance of finding the proton in either of the two positions between the oxygen atoms.

An actual crystal of ice contains an enormous number of individual hydrogen bonds, and our diffraction experiment gives us information about an average bond: (1) Any particular oxygen atom will almost certainly have two, and only two, hydrogens covalently bonded to it at distances of about 1.0 Å. (2) Between any particular pair of neighboring oxygen atoms there will be one, and only one, proton. (3) The positions of the protons throughout the whole ice crystal are *disordered*, so as to yield the structurally averaged arrangement described. An anomaly in the entropy value for ice had been known for some years before Pauling suggested in 1935 that it might be explained by this structural disorder. His explanation was confirmed, twenty years later, by the neutron diffraction study.

The hydrogen-bonded structure of ice (Fig. 6.1b) means that each water molecule makes contact with only four neighbors, and not with the much larger number, 12, that would obtain if the structure were close-packed. This is in fact a very "open" structure, with a lot of unoccupied space between the molecules. That is why the density is so low.

When any crystalline substance melts, the molecules relinquish their overall regularity. The liquid has a more random arrangement of the units. However, on the average, the molecules are about as close together as in the solid. Though our knowledge of the detailed arrangement of the molecules in liquids is tentative, we believe that some degree of local orderliness persists (page 17). The immediate neighbors of any particular molecule are likely to be arranged in the same regular way as they would be in the crystal, but the regularity is confined to small and transient groups of molecules. In the case of water this means that there is a considerable amount of hydrogen bonding of the kind shown in Fig. 6.1b; most molecules will have only four nearest neighbors. This is a strict rule in ice, so that the open, hydrogen-bonded structure runs throughout the crystal. In liquid water the rule may be broken from time to time, so that strictly regular, hydrogen-bonded clusters extend only over small regions. Nevertheless, this accounts for the low density of water and for the enhanced attraction between its molecules, which causes the latent heat of vaporization and surface tension to be high. The partially ice-like structure of water is open, and the molecules are less closely packed than in a normal liquid; hence the density is low. And before a molecule can escape, hydrogen bonds must be broken; hence an abnormal latent heat must be absorbed.

This picture of conditions in liquid water also leads to an understanding of why its density changes in an anomalous way with temperature. A rise of temperature always causes a more vigorous commotion of the molecules of any substance; they need more room, so that the substance has a lower density. This tendency is present in all substances, but in water it meets an opposing tendency. The gradual breakdown, with rising temperature, of the unusually open structure would, by itself, cause the molecules to take up less room, and hence would cause the substance to have a higher density. The balance between these opposing trends leads to an initial increase of density; from 0 to 4°C the breakdown of structure is dominant. Above 4° the increasingly vigorous molecular motion gradually gets the upper hand and the density diminishes, though at a smaller rate than that of a normal liquid.

The high specific heat of water follows from the need to break hydrogen bonds as the temperature is raised. More heat therefore needs to be supplied than to a normal liquid. Another way to look at this same effect is via the concept of *entropy*. Entropy can be regarded as a measure of the disorder of a system. As the temperature rises, the entropy of any substance also rises, corresponding to the increasing disorder as the molecules move around more vigorously. In the case of water there is an unusually marked rise in entropy because to the normal increase is added an extra increase due to breakdown of the well-ordered hydrogen-bonded structure. A high entropy increment per degree rise of temperature implies a high heat input, and hence a high specific heat.

Thus we see that the changes which occur as we change ice just below its melting point to steam just above the boiling point are dominated by the necessity for breaking hydrogen bonds. Ice is completely hydrogen-bonded; liquid water is partially hydrogen-bonded, and diminishingly as the temperature rises; steam consists almost wholly of single molecules, H_2O, without hydrogen bonding. The progressive disorganization and collapse of the hydrogen-bonded structure accounts for the high latent heat of fusion of ice, for the high specific heat of water, and for the high latent heat of evaporation.

The explanation of the high surface tension of water has already been mentioned. Surface tension can be considered as measuring the extra energy possessed by molecules in the surface compared with the generality of molecules in the interior. A molecule inside the liquid makes contact with neighbors in all directions; one at the surface makes no contacts in an outward direction. Work must therefore be done against the intermolecular forces to bring a molecule from the interior to the surface. The stronger the forces, the higher the surface tension. Once again an unusual property of water can be connected with the hydrogen bonding.

water as a solvent The remaining one of the unique properties of water that we wish to discuss is its solvent power, and particularly its power to dissolve salts. Unlike the other properties, this is not so directly connected with the propensity to form hydrogen bonds. But there is an indirect connection: the ability to dissolve salts can be attributed to features of the molecule that also favor hydrogen bonding.

Before any substance can properly dissolve in a liquid, the molecules—or other units—of which the substance is composed must first be torn apart. With salts this is particularly difficult. The ions of which all salts consist carry full positive and negative charges which bind them together strongly. To separate the Na^+ and Cl^- ions of a mole of solid sodium chloride requires an input of about 180 kcal. At ordinary temperatures this can be provided only if there is adequate compensation in the sense that a comparable amount of energy is set free when the separated ions come into contact with the molecules of the solvent.

Water is the only common solvent which can provide this compensation on a scale adequate to enable salts to dissolve. The energy liberated when the separated ions from a mole of sodium chloride enter water is about 179 kcal. This liberation nearly enough balances the energy input, and so the salt is soluble. Though all salts are not soluble in it, water is the best solvent in general. If a salt is to dissolve at all, water will be the most likely solvent because it can sustain ions.

By the same token, molecules which may ionize, but do not necessarily do so, will be encouraged to ionize when dissolved in water. Pure hydrogen chloride is an un-ionized, covalent compound which becomes ionic when dissolved in water according to the equation

$$HCl + H_2O \rightarrow H_3O^+ + Cl^-$$

(We note that the so-called "hydrogen ion" in water is certainly hydrated by combining with one or more molecules of the solvent. The H_3O^+ shown is the simplest possibility, and it is often termed an *oxonium* or *hydronium* ion.) Acetic acid is slightly ionized when dissolved in water, and hence it behaves as a weak acid, whereas in benzene or paraffin it is not ionized at all.

Energy is liberated on an appropriately large scale when ions dissolve in water because the ions combine strongly with water molecules; they become *hydrated*. We have already mentioned this tendency (pages 40 and 95), which is also shown in an extreme form in the conversion, just described, of the true hydrogen ion—the proton—into the oxonium ion. It arises from the polar character of the water molecule, whose negative and positive regions are respectively attracted by positive and negative ions with formation of ion-dipole bonds, which may sometimes develop into dative covalences. This is the chemical explanation of the solvent power of water for ions.

There is also an alternative, physical explanation, and it is instructive to see how the two are really equivalent, as they must be if both are true. According to the inverse-square law, two bodies carrying opposite electrostatic charges $+e$ and $-e$ attract one another with a force equal to e^2/d^2, where d is the distance between them. The law in this form applies strictly only when the two bodies are in a vacuum, though in air the difference is usually negligible. However, when some more substantial medium separates them, the law must be restated in the form:

$$\text{Force} = \frac{e^2}{d^2\epsilon}$$

where ϵ is the *dielectric constant* of the medium. This constant is just a measure of the effectiveness of the medium in diminishing the electrostatic attraction. For water it has the abnormally high value of about 80, which may be compared with 2.3 for benzene or 1.0 for a vacuum.

Thus the high dielectric constant of water reduces the attraction between oppositely charted ions of a salt to little more than 1% of what it would otherwise be and therefore facilitates the separation of the ions which must occur when a salt goes into solution. When we ask *how* water is able to have this effect, the answer is that the water molecule, being dipolar, tends to orient itself when it approaches the ion and, if it gets close enough, to combine with the ion in the hydration process. The intense field of force at the surface of the ion is absorbed by the water molecules and emerges at the outside of the hydration sheath greatly attenuated. Here we are back again at our chemical explanation.

Water is also a good solvent for other polar molecules, provided they are not too large. Organic compounds which consist substantially of carbon and hydrogen (such as benzene C_6H_6 or the paraffins C_nH_{2n+2}) are insoluble in water. But when one or more of the hydrogen atoms is replaced by such groups as —OH, —NH$_2$, or —COOH, the molecule becomes polar and the compound is soluble in water.

The more such groups there are in the molecule, the more soluble the compound is likely to be. The sugars are a good example: their biological function is to provide moderate-sized molecules, often having six or twelve carbon atoms, which are still very soluble in water because they carry a large number of hydroxyl groups. The solubility of such polar molecules can be connected with attractive forces between the polar groups and the water molecules, probably via hydrogen bonds. The biological importance of this is evident: substances consisting of small, polar molecules may dissolve readily in the body fluids, which are mainly water, and can thus be transported to a site where they can be assembled to form large molecules which are no longer soluble.

A factor that tends to make a liquid a good solvent is a low molecular weight. From a practical point of view, we usually reckon the concentration of a solution by the weight of solute contained in a given weight (or volume) of solvent. From the "molecules' point of view" a more proper measure is the number of molecules of solute relative to the number of molecules of solvent.

Hence, if the molecular weight of the solvent is low and that of the solute high, a given molecular ratio (solute/solvent) corresponds to a high weight ratio. An example may help: a 5%, by weight, solution of cane sugar ($C_{12}H_{22}O_{11}$, mol. wt. = 342) in water has a molecular ratio of $5/342:95/18 = 0.0027:1$. If we now change to the solvent alcohol (C_2H_6O, mol. wt. = 46), this same molecular ratio corresponds only to a solution of about 2% by weight, as the reader should check for himself. In this sense—and other things being equal—it is easier to dissolve a given weight of a solute in water than in alcohol.

However, solubility is affected by temperature; nearly always it increases with rise of temperature. Therefore, for good solvent power we need a liquid of low molecular weight and we also need a high temperature. But these conditions tend to be mutually exclusive. Solvents of low molecular weight have low boiling points and cease to be liquids long before even a moderate temperature can be attained. Once again we find water to be unique. Apart from a few elementary substances like helium or hydrogen, it has almost the lowest possible molecular weight; and yet, owing to the hydrogen bonding it remains liquid up to a surprisingly high temperature.

We have now interpreted the more important peculiarities of the substance water in terms of the structure and properties of the molecule, H_2O. This structure and these properties derive from special and peculiar features of the oxygen and hydrogen atoms. As Henderson might have put it, they are uniquely fitted to form a compound with properties uniquely fitted for the support of life.

oxygen
We have already discussed the remarkable properties of the oxygen molecule (page 89), and in particular its surprising reactivity. This is a fact of vast importance in biology and in biological evolution. Because of the high reactivity, the primitive atmosphere could have contained very little oxygen. Primitive forms of life had to make use of the carbon dioxide, which would be present in much larger proportions. By so doing they gradually changed the composition of the atmosphere to a larger proportion of oxygen. Thus more efficient mechanisms dependent on oxidative processes for their energy requirements were able to develop.

The favorable properties of the oxygen atom need not be discussed explicitly. They are implied in our discussions of the various compounds of oxygen.

carbon dioxide
Carbon dioxide, CO_2, is the ultimate source of the carbon atoms in all forms of life. Its utilization depends on the facts that it is a gas, that it is readily soluble in water, and that, when dissolved, it forms a weak acid, carbonic acid.

In the periodic table carbon and silicon are closely related elements. Both are normally quadrivalent. So the contrast between the formally similar oxides CO_2 and SiO_2 is striking. Silica crystallizes in several forms, but all are substances of great hardness with high melting points and zero solubility in water. The reason for this recalcitrant behavior is revealed by a study of crystal structure: in each form of silica we have an arrangement in which every silicon atom is joined to four different oxygens and every oxygen to two different silicons. The structure is indeed formally analogous to that of ice (see Fig. 6.1), but there is the important difference that all the atoms in silica are joined by strong covalent bonds, while in ice the water molecules are joined by relatively much weaker hydrogen bonds.

Silica thus has an "infinite" structure of the kind suggested by Fig. 6.2a. This diagram is schematic only; it does not literally correspond to the structure of any of the forms of silica, which have rings of 6 or 12 atoms, and not of 8 atoms all lying in a plane as would appear from the figure. The whole crystal of silica is really a single "giant molecule," strongly bonded, so that a hard, insoluble material is to be expected. The molecule is $(SiO_2)_n$, where n is the total number of SiO_2 units in the crystal. For a piece of quartz weighing 62 g the molecular weight would be about 36×10^{24}, that is, 62 times the Avogadro number.

Theoretically, carbon dioxide might adopt the same structural pattern. It could do so without violating the normal valence rules for carbon and oxygen. In fact it forms small, discrete molecules shown in Fig. 6.2b. This we can attribute to the ability of carbon to form strong and stable double bonds (page 47). The ability is largely confined to elements of the first short period, and although there may be some tendency for double-bond formation among the elements of the second short period, it is there much weaker. Because carbon can form stable double bonds, its quadrivalence is satisfied in a single CO_2 unit, as distinct from the infinite SiO_2 structure. Therefore, since the molecule is small and light, carbon dioxide exists as a gas at normal temperatures.

The solubility of carbon dioxide in water is considerable. At 15°, water dissolves its own volume of the gas when it is at a pressure of one atmosphere. This fact is due partly to the reaction that carbon dioxide undergoes with water to yield carbonic acid:

figure 6.2

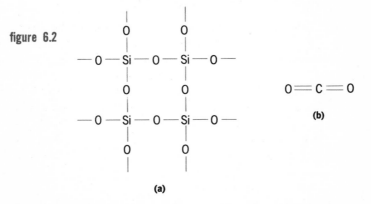

(a)

(b)

Contrasting bonding systems in (a) silicon dioxide and (b) carbon dioxide.

$$CO_2 + H_2O \rightleftharpoons H_2CO_3$$

This acid is a weak one which ionizes slightly in the senses

$$H_2CO_3 + 2H_2O \rightleftharpoons H_3O^+ + HCO_3^- + H_2O \rightleftharpoons 2H_3O^+ + CO_3^-$$

One outcome of this is that the effective solubility of carbon dioxide increases as the aqueous medium becomes more alkaline; the ionization equilibria move farther to the right as the hydrogen ion concentration diminishes, or as the pH value rises.

The primary act in the natural synthesis of all organic materials is the conversion of CO_2 dissolved in the cell fluid of green plants and H_2O into some sort of carbohydrate molecule.* Therefore, the relatively high solubility of carbon dioxide is of the greatest biological importance. The possibility of varying the effective solubility by changing the pH value of the fluid is a valuable control device. This is especially sensitive because the solubility varies rapidly in the region of pH 7, which is commonly found in the fluids of living organisms. This happens because the first dissociation constant (pK) of carbonic acid happens to lie near 7, which is another example of the fitness of the environment.

Henderson's conclusion
We end this chapter and book with a quotation of the final sentences from Henderson's "Fitness of the Environment"

The properties of matter and the course of cosmic evolution are now seen to be intimately related to the structure of the living being and to its activities; they become, therefore, far more important in biology than has been previously suspected. For the whole evolutionary process, both cosmic and organic, is one and the biologist may now rightly regard the universe in its very essence as biocentric.

---

* This does not occur as a single, direct reaction, but as a series of reactions involving complex molecules as intermediaries.

appendix
some standard molecular
units in biochemistry

sugars Carbohydrates were so called because their formulas can usually be cast into the form $C_n(H_2O)_m$. The most important example is *glucose*, which belongs to the group of *hexose* sugars, for which $n = m = 6$. Most carbohydrates have molecules based on a chain of —CH(OH)— groups. The molecule of a hexose, for example, is based on the chain,

$$CH_2OH \cdot CH(OH) \cdot CH(OH) \cdot CH(OH) \cdot CH(OH) \cdot CHO$$

There are four asymmetric carbon atoms, each of which can have alternative configurations, so that a large number of isomeric hexoses can exist. Glucose is one possibility. The molecule normally forms itself into a six-membered ring. This can be considered to occur by the addition, and subsequent removal, of a molecule of water, as follows:

$$CH_2(OH) \cdot CH(OH) \cdot CH(OH) \cdot CH(OH) \cdot CH(OH) \cdot CHO \ + \ H_2O$$
$$\longrightarrow \ CH_2(OH) \cdot CH(OH) \cdot CH(OH) \cdot CH(OH) \cdot CH(OH) \cdot CH(OH)_2$$
$$CH_2(OH) \cdot CH(OH) \cdot CH(OH) \cdot CH(OH) \cdot CH(OH) \cdot CH(OH)_2$$
$$\longrightarrow \ CH_2(OH) \cdot CH \cdot CH(OH) \cdot CH(OH) \cdot CH(OH) \cdot CH \cdot (OH) \ + \ H_2O$$
$$\underline{\qquad\qquad O \qquad\qquad}$$

The actual stereochemistry of the resulting ring molecule was described on page 10, formula (15).

By a similar elimination of water, two or more hexose units may link themselves together to form polysaccharides. Cane sugar, $C_{12}H_{22}O_{11}$, results from the union of molecules of glucose and fructose. By condensation of a large number of glucose units, *starch* and *cellulose* are formed.

Another important sugar is *ribose*, $C_5H_{10}O_5$, whose molecule has a five-membered ring with the structure represented by (1). This

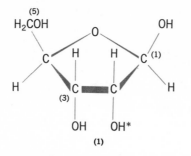

(1)

sugar plays an essential role in the molecule of a nucleic acid, where it may occur either in the form shown or as *deoxyribose*, in which the hydroxyl group marked with an asterisk has been replaced by a hydrogen atom.

In biological systems carbohydrates have two principal functions. The simpler molecules, which are very soluble in water because of their multiplicity of hydroxyl groups, act as "fuels" providing a rapidly available supply of energy. Polysaccharides constitute reserves of fuel in the form of starch or act as structural material in the form of cellulose. These functions are not unrelated.

fats and lipids A carboxylic acid, RCOOH, in whose molecule R is a long hydrocarbon chain, is known as a *fatty acid*. Stearic acid, $C_{17}H_{35}COOH$, is an example (see page 72). *Glycerol* is a triple alcohol with formula $CH_2OH \cdot CHOH \cdot CH_2OH$. *Fats* are compounds formed by union of molecules of glycerol and fatty acids with elimination of water between the hydroxyl group of the alcohol and the carboxyl group of the acid. *Tristearin*, for example, has the formula (2). Fats act as reserve food stores in many animals and in the seeds of plants. In physiologically more active sites lipids appear in the form of *phosphatides*. In the phosphatide molecule one of the hydroxyl groups of the glycerol is engaged with a phosphate ester, as in formula (3), where R' may be a choline residue.

$$H_2CO \cdot CO \cdot C_{17}H_{35}$$
$$|$$
$$HCO \cdot CO \cdot C_{17}H_{35}$$
$$|$$
$$H_2CO \cdot CO \cdot C_{17}H_{35}$$

(2)

$$H_2CO \cdot CO \cdot C_{17}H_{35}$$
$$|$$
$$HCO \cdot CO \cdot C_{17}H_{35}$$
$$|$$
$$H_2CO \cdot PO_2 \cdot OR'$$

(3)

amino acids   Formally these have molecules of the type (4), where R is a hydrogen atom in the case of glycine but some organic group in all the other amino acids. These molecules normally exist in the zwitterion form shown in (5). All except the glycine molecule contain an asymmetric carbon atom, so that the compounds are optically active. In the naturally occurring amino acids the configuration is invariably that of the L series (see page 13). If we imagine ourselves to be viewing the molecule along the H—C direction, we should see the aspect sketched in (6); going round in a clockwise sense, we should see the NH_3^+, the CO_2^-, and the R groups in that order.

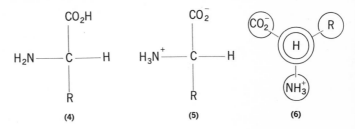

Because they have small, and highly polar, molecules, amino acids are easily soluble in water, but they readily join themselves together via the peptide linkage to form large and very complex protein molecules (see page 110).

nucleosides   Nucleosides are formed by union of a molecule of ribose or deoxy-
and   ribose with a molecule of an organic base. The union occurs by
nucleotides   elimination of water between the NH group of the base and the OH group at position 1 in formula (1). Nucleotides have in addition a phosphoric acid residue, attached in a similar manner at position 3. The parts played by these units in nucleic acids are described on page 115. When one nucleotide molecule is joined to the phosphoric acid residue of another in the nucleic acid chain, the linkage is via the hydroxyl group at position 5.

index